Edward Foley

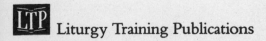

Rites
of Religious
Profession

Pastoral Introduction and Complete Text

LTP Liturgy Training Publications

Copyright © 1989, Archdiocese of Chicago. All rights reserved. Liturgy Training Publications, 1800 North Hermitage Avenue, Chicago IL 60622-1101; 312/486-7008.

Cover and design: Ana M. Stephenson.
Cover art: "Untitled Stuffer Rug" designed and woven by Margaret Windeknecht. Used with permission of the artist.

Printed in the United States of America.
ISBN 0-929650-01-8

TO MY CAPUCHIN BROTHERS

Contents

Abbreviations

CSEL   Corpus Scriptorum Ecclesiasticorum Latinorum

CSL   Constitution on the Sacred Liturgy

DCC   Dogmatic Constitution on the Church

DENZ.   H. Denzinger, *Enchiridion Symbolorum Definitionum et Declarationum de Rebus Fidei et Morum.* 36th ed. by A. Schönmetzer. Freiburg im Br.: Herder, 1976

DOL   *Documents on the Liturgy 1963–1979: Conciliar, Papal and Curial Texts.* Collegeville: Liturgical Press, 1982

EACW   Environment and Art in Catholic Worship

FP   Florilegium Patristicum

GCD   General Catechetical Directory

GILH   General Instruction of the Liturgy of the Hours

GIRM	General Instruction of the Roman Missal
MCW	Music in Catholic Worship, rev. ed.
PG	Migne, Patrologia, series graeca
PL	Migne, Patrologia, series latina
RCIA	Rite of Christian Initiation of Adults
RFR	Roman Franciscan Rite of Religious Profession
RRL	Decree on the Up-to-Date Renewal of Religious Life
RRP	Rite of Religious Profession
VC II	*Vatican Council II*, ed. Austin Flannery. Collegeville: Liturgical Press, 1975

Introduction

L ong before the Rite of Christian Initiation of Adults (RCIA) made its official debut in 1972, religious life and its initiatory rituals were considered to be inextricably linked with baptism. This ancient bond is confirmed both by the consistent testimony of our past and the contemporary teaching of the church. Thus, the Dogmatic Constitution on the Church (DCC) acknowledges that religious life and religious profession are grounded in Christian baptism,[1] and the Rite of Religious Profession (RRP) notes in its opening sentence:

> Many Christians, in response to God's call, dedicate themselves . . . by the sacred bonds of religious life, desiring to follow Christ more closely through the evangelical counsels so that the grace of baptism may be more fruitful in them.[2]

Though this link between baptism and the vowed life has been recognized since the emergence of the first religious communities, the past few years have witnessed a renewed interest in this relationship. In part, this is a result of the general renewal of religious life mandated by the Second Vatican Council.[3] To a large extent, however, the first stages of this postconciliar renewal of religious life concentrated on the rediscovery and reappropriation of the founding spirit and goals of individual communities. A broad appreciation for religious life in its baptismal context, on the other hand, seems to be more directly related to the promulgation of the RCIA.

Since 1972, this revolutionary document has served a variety of religious communities in a number of ways. There is a growing appreciation on the part of many religious for the pastoral theology embodied in the RCIA, as well as a developing reliance on the processes and rituals outlined in these rites. Thus, some have shaped individual liturgies of investiture or profession according to the models found in the RCIA, while others have developed entire formation programs according to the processes outlined therein.

Though there are many similarities between initiation into the Christian community and initiation into religious life, it is also true that these are quite different phenomena. The former, which can properly be called ecclesial initiation, is the foundational and definitive act of entry into the whole of the Christian mystery. Climaxing in the sacraments of baptism, confirmation and eucharist, ecclesial initiation is the process whereby the elect

> are admitted into the people of God. They are graced with adoption as children of God and are led by the Holy Spirit into the promised fullness of time begun in Christ and, as they share in the eucharistic sacrifice and meal, even to a foretaste of the kingdom of God.[4]

Initiation into a religious community, on the other hand, is a specifying process that concretely defines a context for living out this baptismal commitment in poverty, chastity and obedience. It is by adhering to these evangelical counsels, in the founding spirit and living charism of a specific community, that religious women and men define their baptismal commitment and mission in the church. Therefore, initiation into a religious community presumes and builds upon the first Christian vocation articulated in ecclesial initiation.

Because of the intimate relationship between ecclesial initiation and initiation into religious life, there can and should be a mutual influence between these two types of initiation. As the RCIA has already influenced contemporary thinking and practice for Christian marriage, reconciliation and parish renewal,[5] it most assuredly can enrich the rites and processes of religious initiation. Conversely, the renewal of religious life in this postconciliar period has resulted in certain developments, such as the refinement of apostolic formation programs, which could be beneficial for the ongoing development of the RCIA.

There is a difference, however, between healthy influence and indiscriminate borrowing, between carefully adapting and baldly adopting theological insights, formational processes or liturgical celebrations one from another. Because of the fundamental difference between ecclesial initiation and initiation into a religious community, the theology, processes or rites of the one cannot simply be borrowed in their entirety by the other. What is not always clear, however, is the shape that mutual influence and intelligent adaptation can or should take.

The purpose of this volume is to explore the relationship between these two forms of initiation in order to discover how they have influenced each other in the past and how they might enrich each other in the future. More specifically, we are concerned with learning how that pivotal reform embodied in the RCIA, so influential in shaping our understanding of the Christian vocation, might further contribute to our understanding of the process of religious formation and profession.

We will begin with a historical survey. This will outline the origins and development of this relationship (chapter 1). Against this historical background we will explore the sacramental context of religious life and raise the question of the sacramentality of religious profession (chapter 2). Next we will discuss the pastoral implications of the RCIA for religious life, with formational as well as ritual suggestions (chapter 3).

Finally, we will address the ritual planning process (chapter 4) and offer ritual models for perpetual and simple profession rites (chapter 5). Though we do not presume that a final synthesis is necessary or even possible at this time, it is hoped that this study will aid both our reflection and pastoral practice.

This volume includes, as a second part, the entire text of the Rite of Religious Profession (RRP). This was first translated into English by the International Committee on English in the Liturgy and published in 1971 by the United States Catholic Conference. The version presented here has been revised by the Bishops' Committee on the Liturgy to conform to subsequent legislation.

Notes

1. DCC, n. 44.

2. RRP Introduction, n. 1.

3. RRL, n. 1.

4. RCIA, n. 206.

5. As an example of RCIA's influence on marriage, see Kenneth Stevenson, *To Join Together: The Rite of Marriage,* Studies in the Reformed Rites of the Catholic Church 5 (New York: Pueblo Publishing, 1987), 193ff; concerning its influence on penance, see James Lopresti, *Penance: A Reform Proposal for the Rite,* American Essays in Liturgy 6 (Washington, DC: The Pastoral Press, 1987); as to its influence on parish renewal, see Giorgio Zevini, "The Christian Initiation of Adults into the Neo-Catechumenal Community," *Structures of Initiation in Crisis,* ed. Luis Maldonada and David Power, Concilium 122 (New York: Seabury Press, 1979), 65–74.

An Overview of the History

There are numerous published histories of religious life that adequately chart the origins and development of almost every imaginable aspect of this phenomenon.[1] Even a brief summary of this complex history would be impossible here. The more modest goal of this chapter is to outline some salient points of contact between Christian initiation and religious life over the centuries. This relatively narrow and condensed historical sketch will provide the context for the theological and pastoral discussions that follow.

The New Testament Period

In the earliest days of Christianity there was no "religious life" as we know it today: There was also no need for it. The churches had enormous diversity in practice and theology, but it seems clear that the early believers considered themselves to be the eschatological community; the universal means for entering this community was baptism.[2] Apart from this there was no separate group of elect, no inner circle that controlled any revelation or private vision of the mystery.

It is true that the "twelve," by virtue of their experience of the Jesus of history, were held in particular esteem as were other "apostles," such as Paul. Besides the twelve and apostles, we can identify different groups or "orders"[3] in the various communities: widows (Acts 6:1), deacons (Philemon 1:1), elders (Acts 11:30), orphans (James 1:27) and helpers (1 Corinthians 13:28). Some of these are recognizable because of a certain task or charism, others through a particular need or gift. Despite the existence of such groups, the call to discipleship and the promise of salvation were clearly not the exclusive prerogative of a select few but were extended equally to all in Jesus Christ.

Two groups that significantly influenced the evolution of religious life were widows and virgins. As is clear from the language of the first letter to Timothy (5:3, 9), widows were a recognized and restricted order in the ancient church. Not every woman who lost a husband was admitted to their ranks. Specific standards and requirements (1 Timothy 5:9–10) demonstrate that the "true widows" exemplified the Christian ideal.[4] One important part of this exemplification was undoubtedly the celibate life that these widows accepted. Such women played an important role in the early community, were sometimes considered part of the clergy[5] and in the East seem to have evolved into the order of deaconess.[6]

Of the group known as virgins, Benedictine scholar Jean Leclercq remarks:

> The existence during the first centuries of the Church of Christian women who lived in voluntary virginity for God is an important fact in the history of the origins of the religious life. . . . It is known that in the Graeco-Roman Christian world these virgins existed and constituted a separate and in some way sacred category. At the time of monasticism's birth, a free commitment, no doubt often distinct from baptism and thenceforth final, was an established fact. There is no evidence of an

explicit commitment of the same kind concerning men, the ascetics and confessors.[7]

Though Leclercq correctly notes the importance of dedicated virgins to the history of religious life, his reconstruction needs to be read with a certain caution. For example, it is undeniable that groups of women other than widows lived in voluntary virginity in the early Christian community.[8] There is also sufficient evidence to conclude that certain Christian men of the same epoch were similarly committed to virginity,[9] though there is little convincing evidence that such men ever shared any kind of common life. Furthermore, though a life of voluntary celibacy could be considered as distinct from baptism, it is also necessary to stress its continuity with baptism.

We already see in Paul's letters the close connection that the early community made between virginity and the fullness of the baptismal commitment (1 Corinthians 7:32–35). Various gospel texts, as well, though recognizing that voluntary celibacy is a special gift, nonetheless acknowledge the strong link between virginity and the kingdom into which all baptized are invited (Matthew 19:12). One author would go so far as to conclude that "during the first centuries of the church, the ceremony of initiation into the Christian mysteries was closely associated with the maintenance of perfect chastity."[10] Clearly a commitment to celibacy in the early community could not have arisen from any other call but baptism and was, in turn, valued as an eschatological sign of what the whole baptized community was to become.

Various groups and ministries existed among the first Christians, but none of these had any special claim to holiness, which was the prerogative and presumption of all those called to follow Jesus. The ordinary response and fulfillment of that call came through baptism. Some men and many more women[11] chose a life of voluntary virginity, but this commitment was intimately wedded to the baptismal vocation.[12]

The Second and Third Centuries

The second and third centuries saw the rise of Christian monasticism. Though its origins are obscure,[13] Christian monasticism was most likely born out of the ascetic tendency to withdraw to the Egyptian desert in pursuit of a life of perfection. Initially, there were no rules or organizations but only isolated hermits who occasionally attached themselves to another ascetic, thus establishing a loose association of anchorites.[14] Despite the somewhat haphazard and individualistic nature of the movement's early years, certain themes about the ascetic life echo through the writings of this era and have had a significant impact on the emergence of religious life.

One such theme sprang from the belief that martyrdom was similar to Christian initiation. This belief developed from the conviction that both initiation and martyrdom transform the believer into Christ. Consequently, martyrdom was thought to be like a second baptism. This was a view held by the Shepherd of Hermas (mid–second century), Justin Martyr (d. around 165), Origen (d. around 254) and especially Tertullian (d. around 225).[15] Some of the same sources draw a parallel between the martyr's suffering and the ascetic life and consider the latter to be a kind of martyrdom.[16] Once these two equations had been established (martyrdom is a second baptism; the ascetic life is spiritual martyrdom), it was a small step to suggesting that the ascetic life was a kind of second baptism. This determinative perspective, which might have first been expressed by a fourth-century group of Syrian ascetics known as Messalians,[17] clearly emerged by the fifth century.

Also important in this period was the embryonic belief that commitment to an ascetic way of life was "sacramental" (a *musterion*) and entailed the forgiveness of sins.[18] Athanasius (d. 373) seems to have alluded to such a "sacramental effect" when, in his biography of Antony the Hermit (d. 356) he wrote, "The Lord has wiped clean the items dating from his birth, but from the time he became a monk, and devoted himself to God, you can take an account."[19] As adult baptisms declined and the church became more concerned about the postbaptismal reconciliation of sinners, this connection between the ascetic life and the remission of sin grew in importance.

The Fourth to the Sixth Centuries

With the Edict of Milan in 313, Christianity acquired legal status in the empire and entered a period of relative peace and imperial cooperation. This new relationship radically transformed both the empire and the church; within a century the church of the martyrs became an imperial church. Particularly important for the development of cenobitic monasticism, which became the dominant form of religious life during this period,[20] was the surge of new members into the church. This influx of new members was a direct result of the imperial favor and consequent social acceptability that the fourth-century church enjoyed. In this context, it is possible to understand monasticism as a counterbalance to the expansion of the church and the dilution of baptismal fervor. As Jaroslav Pelikan summarizes:

> Monasticism of the fourth and fifth centuries was a protest, in the name of the authentic teaching of Jesus, against . . . the secularization of the church and the lowering of the standard of discipleship set in the gospels.[21]

Though monasticism-as-protest is by no means a complete explanation of the expansion during this period, it does identify one important stimulus. Put in gentler terms, "at the end of the age of martyrs, the first monks expressed the radical requirements of the kingdom in relation to a community that was no longer called to heroism."[22]

This more heroic form of Christianity received newfound meaning with the cessation of persecution under Constantine. The end of persecution meant the disappearance of martyrs; when this prized form of "second baptism" was no longer available to the committed Christian, the "spiritual martyrdom" of monastic life became the appropriate substitute.

Monks became the new martyrs, and because martyrdom was already synonymous with second baptism, the new martyrs became the new baptized. It was Jerome (d. 420) who first referred to monastic life as "a kind of second baptism."[23] This connection between monastic life and baptism soon gave way to an explicit belief in the superiority of the former over the latter. At the beginning of the sixth century, for example, Pseudo-Dionysius wrote: "Of all the initiates, the most exalted order is the sacred rank of the monks which has been purified of all stain and possess full power and complete holiness in its own activities."[24] He further suggested that the process of monastic initiation was itself "sacramental."[25]

Also significant during this period was the evolving identification of monastic life with second penance. By the second century the Christian community had been confronted with the problem of those who committed serious sin after baptism, which could be considered first penance. In writers such as the Shepherd of Hermas we find early evidence of an institutional response to this dilemma in the form of "second penance." This tradition evolved over the centuries into public canonical penance, tariff penance and eventually "confession" in the Western church. Initially, however, forgiveness was thought to be available only once after baptism. Penance then became a lifelong obligation. This belief was important for the development of religious life. From at least the fifth century, there were those who held that:

> Religious life is a form of private penance and as such is a fully equivalent substitute for ecclesiastical penance. Its starting point is the *conversio* by which a person binds himself by a vow . . . to a life of perpetual penance in prayer, mortification, sexual abstinence, etc., and manifests externally in his dress the exchange of the secular for the religious life. . . . Despite the arduousness of the commitment that it involves, *conversio* was an easier state than that of public penance . . . and for this reason it tended more and more to replace it.[26]

Thus, religious life not only replaced martyrdom as the new equivalent to second baptism, but it also became an accepted form of second penance. This development took on even more importance in the centuries following the peace of Constantine with the gradual decline in adult baptism; the subsequent rise of infant baptism and the consequent growth of second penance.

The evolution of monasticism as a seemingly superior form of Christian life not only meant the displacement of baptism in theology and practice but also entailed the borrowing and adaptation of baptismal processes and rituals. For example, an extensive preparation period or catechumenate was common before the baptism of adults.

> In a similar way the monks seem to have realized gradually the need for further testing and instruction of candidates. . . . Cassian [d. around 435] already knows of the full year under an elder's direction, but he still places it after profession. By the beginning of the sixth century, the Western practice required a full year's training before investiture with the habit.[27]

Besides the development of a specific period of preparation before full acceptance into the community, this era also witnessed the emergence of vow formulas. Over the centuries, these formulas came to be considered as synonymous with the act of religious profession. Though initiation into religious life has, in a sense, traditionally involved a "profession," this has not always been equivalent to the making of vows.[28] At the birth of religious life there were no vows, and the beginning of what could be considered a religious or monastic life was simply marked "by the renouncement of goods and the abandonment of the earthly city."[29] The visible sign of this renunciation eventually became the donning of the religious habit.

It is possible that an oral pronouncement of vows was required as early as the time of Basil (d. 379)[30] and a formula of profession probably was in existence by the middle of the fifth century.[31] The emergence of such a formula demonstrates that the baptismal vows, which were once sufficient for living the ascetic life,[32] were no longer adequate, and a further formulation was required. Ironically, these first formulas probably consisted of a series of questions and answers,[33] similar to the ancient baptismal texts.

A relatively formal initiatory process is outlined in the sixth century *Rule of the Master,* which includes an examination, renunciation of goods, prayer, declaration of the freedom and willingness to stay, and the sign of peace (chapter 89). Benedict's *Rule,* written after the *Rule of the Master,* outlines a process that includes a written and publicly sworn promise of stability, fidelity and obedience (which was strikingly similar to baptismal promises),[34] a psalm verse, prostration and prayers, and the vesting with the habit (chapter 58).

It is from this period that we also find formalized rituals for the dedication of virgins. The first of these, which survives as a description of the dedication of Marcellina, the sister of Ambrose (d. 397), consists of a short prayer, a longer text in the form of a eucharistic prayer and the giving of the veil by the bishop.[35] Though some would suggest that these rituals were borrowed from marriage rites and not baptismal rites, it is probable that the commitment to virginity itself was much more in imitation of the sacrament of baptism than of marriage, which was not considered "sacramental" at this time.[36]

There was also a shift in terminology during this era. The term *consecratio* rather than *velatio* or *benedictio,* for example, was used to designate the liturgical ceremonies for the initiation of virgins in the fourth century;[37] the term *religiosa* appears in Gaul in the sixth century;[38] and Gregory the Great (d. 604) employed the terms *virgines sacrae* and *virgines sacratae.*[39] Odo Casel would contend that, even before such changes in terminology, the concept of virginal dedication or monastic profession as *consecratio* was prevalent in early Eastern monasticism.[40]

In summarizing the developments of this epoch, Jaroslav Pelikan remarks:

> Thus there was introduced into the life and teaching of the church a double standard of discipleship, based on a bifurcation of the ethical demands of Jesus into "commandments," which

"imply necessity" and which were taken to be binding upon everyone, and "counsels of perfection," which were "left to choice" and which ultimately were binding only upon the monastic athletes. . . . [Therefore] the meaning of perfection was increasingly to be sought not in the family life and daily work of the Christian believer within society, but in the life of the monk and the nun, to whom the word *religious* applied in a strict sense as a technical term.[41]

Furthermore, with the decline of infant baptism, the preclusion of marriage as a sacrament and the secondary place of presbyteral ordination during this period, monastic profession emerged as the primary adult ritual for initiation into a life of perfection. By the seventh century we find evidence of the belief that monastic life was a kind of second baptism and the further claim that the profession of vows itself was a ritual of second baptism.[42]

The Early Middle Ages [600–1100]

The transition from the ancient world to the Middle Ages saw no decline in the post-Constantinian trend to value the vowed life over that of the lay state. The cloistered life was seen more and more as the privileged state in the church, superior to anything that the world could offer. Common now was the belief that religious profession was equivalent to second baptism.[43] Some writers of this period went so far as to teach that entry into the cloister was even more important than baptism.[44] For others, especially in the East, monastic profession was thought to be sacramentally equivalent to baptism. The renowned abbot Theodore the Studite (d. 826), influenced by the thought of Pseudo-Dionysius, taught that monastic profession was an authentic *musterion (sacramentum)*, like baptism and eucharist, and was founded upon apostolic tradition.[45]

A natural consequence of this exaggerated view of religious life was a distinct detachment from and contempt for the world. This attitude eventually found articulation in the phrase "the angelic life," which became the most appropriate summary of the monastic way.[46] The cloister thus came to be considered as the "antichamber to heaven,"[47] and the eschatological community no longer encompassed all the baptized, but only those in vows. Benedict himself seems to have preserved "this fundamental conviction that the monk is a fully initiated Christian living his Christian life in a community which imitates that early community life spoken of in the Acts of the Apostles."[48]

It is noteworthy that the monastic state was commonly valued over the clerical state. Already John Chrysostom (d. 407) had demonstrated a "distrustful attitude" toward priesthood,[49] and Pseudo-Dionysius believed that monks were at the summit of the hierarchy of initiates (or at the level of perfection) while priests were only second in the rank of initiators (or at the level of illumination).[50] The superiority of monks over clergy and laity was dramatically articulated by Abbo of Fleury (d. 1004), who first noted that there were three degrees of Christians: laity, clergy and monks. He then asserted that the first (lay) was good, the second (clerical) was better and the third (monastic) was excellent.[51]

This preference for religious life over the clerical state was testimony to an age in which monasticism dominated the Western church. Such domination resulted, in part, from the various monastic reforms in the West, through which "the monastic conquest of the church sought to make itself ever more complete."[52] Then, for a variety of reasons, monks began to be ordained priests and by the beginning of the ninth century more than a third of all monks were priests or deacons.[53] Even so, it is appropriate to consider this era as the apogee of monasticism's influence. Such is demonstrated in the victory of monastic celibacy over the episcopacy in the East and over the presbyterate in the West.

Many ritual developments in this period demonstrate a continuity with and a superseding of baptismal rituals. Profession scrutinies at the Benedictine foundation of Monte Cassino, for example, followed the pattern of baptismal scrutinies, and sometimes the new monk wore his cowl the day of profession in imitation of the neophytes who wore a covering *(chrismale)* on the day of their baptism to protect the chrism.[54] Besides the ritual continuity between baptism and religious profession, which was especially apparent in the Eastern church,[55] this era also witnessed the addition of rituals such as the blessing of the habit.[56] These ritual additions, similar to the addition of an oral pronouncement of vows in the previous period, demonstrate that traditional baptismal rituals now seemed inadequate for expressing the significance of initiation into religious life. The latter now required an increasingly distinctive ritualization.

Probably more than in any other period of Christian history, religious life was viewed during the early Middle Ages as the perfect form of Christian initiation. During this period religious profession was so singularly identified with second baptism that the religious probably were no longer even conscious of the fact that second baptism had once referred to martyrdom or by extension to every kind of penance.[57] Religious life had consequently come to usurp not only the role of the baptized as the eschatological community, but also the theology, terminology and in some respects even the rituals of baptism. Ironically, it was also to preserve these things for another era.

The Late Middle Ages [1100–1500]

With the late Middle Ages a dramatic shift occurred in the monastic domination of the Western church. At the beginning of this period Western monasticism enjoyed a renaissance through the reforms of charismatic figures such as Bernard of Clairvaux (d. 1153). Despite this renaissance, monasticism's power began to wane, eventually yielding its preferential position to the clergy. This transformation was the result of a number of complex developments.

One of these was the emergence in the West of a more refined sacramental system, one that did not equate profession with baptism or number it among the sacraments.[58] Also there was a growing emphasis on the importance of the priesthood. This was partially because of the priest's central role in the church's sacraments and was further aided by the birth of groups such as the canon regulars whose spirituality was based on the "exaltation of the priesthood."[59]

In a parallel development, the clericalization of the monasteries, which had begun in a previous period, acquired new momentum. Such clericalization was, in part, a result of the increased demand for Masses, offered as commutations for penance and for the dead. Furthermore, Vandenbroucke suggests that the absorption of monasticism by the clerical state resulted from what he considered to be a lack of a sound theology of confirmation. "As a consequence, once the question of monastic radiation was posed, it was done so in terms of the priesthood, this being better known by its powers and effects."[60] The ultimate consequence of these developments came at the Council of Vienne in 1311, which decreed that as a general rule monks had an obligation to be ordained.[61] Thus priesthood, with its own initiatory processes and rites of tonsure, minor orders, subdiaconate and diaconate, became the new fullness of Christian initiation and the preferred way to perfection.

This progressive displacement of monastic life is further influenced by the appearance of many nonmonastic types of religious life during this period. These did much to redefine the nature of religious life. The Augustinian canons, who became the dominant form of canons regular in the twelfth century, developed a more flexible form of community life by basing their life on the so-called Rule of Augustine[62] instead of the Rule of Benedict. Mendicant orders, such as the Franciscans and Dominicans, rejected the regiment and stability of monasticism, and turned to a more apostolic and mobile form of religious life.

Women's communities also underwent significant change in this period. Since the time of Benedict, virtually every community of religious women was cloistered and followed a male monastic rule. Often, monasteries and nunneries existed side by side, and in some instances outstanding abbesses governed both the women's and men's communities.[63] In general, however, religious life for women was controlled by men.[64] Various developments in the late Middle Ages began to counteract though not reverse this trend. The Franciscans and Dominicans, for example, founded communities for women called "second orders" as well as "third orders" for people living in the world. Women who joined the latter were not confined to the cloistered life, which had become the rule for women and which Boniface VIII (d. 1303) had officially imposed on all nuns in 1298.[65] Consequently, women such as Catherine of Siena (d. 1380), who belonged to the Dominican third order, were free to "carry out the ministries for which they were so revered."[66] Also notable in the evolution of women's communities in this period was the beguine movement. Beguines were women (male counterparts were called beghards) who lived in common without vows, dedicated themselves to charitable work and were free to leave the community and marry.[67]

Besides these changes in various women's and men's communities, there also emerged mixed groups of professed and laity such as the order of Grandmont,[68] mixed communities of women and men such as the foundations of Gerhard Groote (d. 1384),[69] and an expanding number of religious who wished to live out their vocation in the world. Moreover, it was during this era that the church came to accept marriage as a sacrament in which the consent of the couple was constitutive of the sacrament.[70] Together such developments created what might be called a climate of "spiritual emancipation of the laity."[71]

The ritual of religious profession in the Middle Ages still maintained some ties with its baptismal origins, but religious communities continued to develop their own repertory of distinctive rituals. This tendency was undoubtedly stimulated by the increasing emphasis on the profession of vows as the determinative act in the definition of a religious and the narrowing focus on poverty, chastity and obedience as the three essential vows.[72]

Consequently, there developed the need to particularize this distinguishing profession ritual and shape it in the perceived image of religious life. Thus, the liturgies of religious profession increasingly drew upon marriage rites for the consecration of virgins, rites of penance for religious profession and funeral liturgies for monastic profession. In ritual as well as theology, the vowed life began to appear less as the ultimate way of perfection or entry into the eschatological community and more as the accepted way to renunciation and the penitential journey. Just as baptism had been eclipsed by profession in a previous era, so was religious profession in the Middle Ages eclipsed by ordination, the new way to full initiation.

1500 to the Present

The 16th century was a time of unusual ferment and change for the church. The Council of Trent (1545–1563) acknowledged that many unacceptable practices and abuses had developed during the medieval period and launched a wide-ranging reform within the church. This reform extended to religious life; in Trent's final session the council offered a number of directives for religious. Boniface VIII's teaching that all nuns should live within an enclosure was reiterated. Abbesses were forbidden to govern monasteries of women and men. Monasteries should be governed only by a member of that same community. Trent also offered guidelines on such varied matters as monthly confession and communion for nuns and the period of probation before profession.[73]

Virtually every major religious community responded to the reforming spirit of this age. Early in the 16th century, for example, a spiritualist reform within the first order Franciscans led to the birth of a new family of observant friars called the Capuchins.[74] In 1562 Teresa of Avila (d. 1582) launched a reform among the second order Carmelites; this was taken up by John of the Cross (d. 1591) among the first order, giving rise to the Discalced Carmelites.[75] In the early 17th century an influential reform community within the Benedictine tradition known as the Congregation of St. Maur was founded in Paris and quickly rose to prominence.[76] In the same century various reforms of the Strict Observance spread throughout the Cistercian Order. At the abbey of Notre-Dame de la Trappe, the dominant strand of this reform emerged as the Trappists.[77]

Besides reforms within well-established orders of the church, this period also witnessed the birth of highly innovative forms of religious life. Determinative in the shaping of many such communities was the adoption of simple rather than solemn vows by some new orders. The difference between solemn and simple vows was first explained by the 12th century canonist Gratian, who used this distinction to show why the marriages of some who had vowed to live perpetual chastity were considered illicit but valid, while others were considered illicit and invalid.[78] The wide acceptance of this distinction eventually led to Boniface VIII's decision that vows taken at the reception of holy orders or in a religious order approved by the Holy See constituted solemn profession.[79]

The first group to challenge successfully this equation was the Society of Jesus founded by Ignatius of Loyola (d. 1556) in 1534. The Jesuits, as they came to be called, adopted an inventive form of religious life that proved to be very successful within a short period of time. This new society was highly centralized, well organized, mobile and free from the confinement of a common liturgical life.[80] Symbolic of this new approach to religious life was the Jesuit adoption of simple rather than solemn vows. The latter, traditionally identified with the cloistered life,[81] had come to symbolize a stability and isolation incompatible with Ignatius's vision for the society. Simple vows, on the other hand, better suited this mobile and original form of religious life.

A growing number of women's communities also attempted a more mobile and apostolic life, though success was often quite difficult. The Franciscan tertiary Angela Merici (d. 1540), for example, established a company of women under the patronage of St. Ursula in 1535. Similar to the beguines, this society initially adopted no religious habit, took no vows and the women engaged in works of charity while living with their families. Though approved by Paul III (d. 1549) in 1544, Trent's subsequent teaching on enclosure for all nuns was difficult to ignore. The influential archbishop of Milan, Charles Borromeo (d. 1584), eventually directed these women to adopt a habit, live a common life and accept enclosure, though in the context of simple vows.[82]

The struggle to avoid enclosure was also unsuccessfully attempted by Francis de Sales (d. 1622) and by Jane Frances de Chantal (d. 1641), who founded the Visitation Order. This group of women lost its struggle to remain an apostolic foundation in simple vows and was forced to become a contemplative and cloistered community.[83] It was Vincent de Paul (d. 1660) and Louise de Marillac (d. 1660) who first successfully established a noncloistered community of religious women after Trent. They achieved this by founding a lay organization without vows in 1633. Nine years later, Vincent de Paul allowed the first women in this community to take vows. Though a few women took perpetual vows with Vincent's permission, he much preferred that they take simple or private vows.[84] This innovation opened the way for innumerable communities of women that followed the Daughters of Charity into the apostolic arena.

It was especially in France that such apostolic women's communities flourished, and by the time of the French Revolution in 1789 more than 30,000 sisters were engaged in charitable work for the church in France. Despite the suppression of all religious orders and congregations in France in 1792, the 19th century was a period of astounding growth for such communities, and by 1900 the number of French sisters in apostolic congregations numbered more than 150,000. Though many of these communities did not initially seek or receive official ecclesiastical status,[85] such was finally extended to many congregations by Leo XIII (d. 1903) in his apostolic constitution, *Conditae a Christo.*[86] It was the 1917 Code of Canon Law that finally recognized all congregations professing simple vows as religious.[87]

Besides the spread of simply professed congregations of women and simply professed clerical congregations of men,[88] this period also saw the rise of independent nonclerical men's communities such as the Christian Brothers, the birth of congregations such as the Paulists whose members make promises but take no public vows,[89] the emergence of secular institutes such as Opus Dei,[90] and more recently the growth of noncanonical groups such as the Sisters for Christian Community.[91] Each of these developments underscores the increasingly apostolic orientation of modern religious life. Thus, religious life after Trent—especially for women—recognizes that mission is fundamental to the religious vocation and is not exclusively a clerical enterprise. This apostolic orientation is reflected in the profession rites of many modern communities, in which the profession of vows or promises is often coupled with the presentation of some insignia of profession. These insignia, such as a ring or a cross, are particularly important expressions of witness for those communities that originated outside the cloister and do not have a specific religious habit.

Summary

Though this brief survey cannot chart all the shifts and evolutions in this complex history, it has outlined some of the fundamental developments that have defined religious life until our own day. In summary, we have seen that virginity, common life and martyrdom were understood very early as some of the symbols of a full response to the baptismal call. When a complete response to this call was not considered possible from the entire Christian community, certain individuals and then groups took it upon themselves to shape a way of life in which these ideals could be most perfectly achieved. Eventually this movement became not just an alternative way for making a full response, but the preferred and finally the only way to respond adequately.

In the process of equating full Christian initiation with religious life, the very rites and processes of adult initiation came to be adapted and preserved in the rites and processes of religious profession. Eventually, however, the emergence of a distinctive ritual vocabulary for initiation into religious life began to overshadow the baptismal thematic in profession rites. In conjunction with a transition of religious life from a way of election to a way of penance, profession was eclipsed by presbyteral ordination as the ultimate Christian ritual of sanctification. This development was supported by the refinement of sacramental theology and an increased call for the celebration of eucharist. Consequently, religious life was displaced as the most perfect Christian state, and priests became the true elect. The stronger apostolic orientation of priesthood further dictated that both the way of perfection and the church's mission became clerical prerogatives.

Recent history has demonstrated a growing unwillingness to accept ordination plus solemn profession as the sole embodiment of the Christian vocation. The increased number of nonclerical groups dedicated to the Christian life through a specific apostolic vision has helped religious life to forge an identity separate from the priesthood. This has contributed to the conviction that the call to holiness and the commitment to mission are not the prerogatives of a select few. Rather, they are fundamental to the baptismal vocation that a growing number of religious are consciously embracing. In so doing, such religious are further upholding the dignity of all the baptized.

Notes

1. Though it is not possible to give even an introductory bibliography on this topic, we offer the following sampling of general works on the history

of Christian monasticism and religious life: P. F. Anson, *Patir au désert: Vingt siècles d'érémitisme* (Paris: Cerf, 1967); Mario Escobar, ed., *Ordini e congregazioni religiose*, 2 vols. (Turin: Società Editrice Internazionale, 1951–53); Max Heimbucher, *Die Orden und Kongregationen der katholischen Kirche*, 2 vols. (Paderborn: Ferdinand Schöningh, 1933–34); W. Hinnebusch, *History of the Dominican Order*, 2 vols. (Staten Island: Alba House, 1966–73); Lázaro Iriarte, *Franciscan History: The Three Orders of St. Francis of Assisi*, trans. Patricia Ross (Chicago: Franciscan Herald Press, 1983); David Knowles, *Christian Monasticism* (New York: McGraw-Hill, 1967); idem, *The Religious Orders in England*, 3 vols. (Cambridge: University Press, 1950); Jean F. Lestocoquoy, *La Vie religieuse en France du VIIe au XXe siècle* (Paris: A. Michel); M. Pacaut, *Les ordres monastiques et religieux au Moyen Age* (Paris: F. Nathan, 1970); Philibert Schmitz, *Histoire de l'ordre de Saint-Benoît*, 7 vols. (Maredsous: Editions de l'Abbaye, 1942–1956).

2. Reginald Fuller, "Christian Initiation in the New Testament," *Made Not Born* (Notre Dame: University of Notre Dame Press, 1976), 11.

3. Order or "ordo" in the ancient sense does not indicate hierarchical distinction or the domination of one group over another but expresses what Nathan Mitchell calls "that particular way of being-in-the-world called church." He continues, "Everyone in the church, including those publicly designated for penance, belongs to an order and exercises a ministry, for there is no such thing . . . as a Christian who lacks an 'order' or ministry." Nathan Mitchell, *Mission and Ministry*, Message of the Sacraments 6 (Wilmington: Michael Glazier, Inc., 1982), 217–18.

4. Roger Gryson, *The Ministry of Women in the Early Church*, trans. Jean Laporte and Mary Louise Hall (Collegeville: The Liturgical Press, 1976), 9.

5. For example, by Tertullian (d. around 225), *De Monogamia* 11.1 (CSEL 76.65).

6. See J. Viteaux, "L'Institution des Diacres et des Veuves," *Revue d'Histoire Ecclésiastique* 22 (1926), 513–36; also, J. Mayer, ed., *Monumenta de viduis, diaconissis virginibusque tractantia*, Florilegium Patristicum 42 (Bonn: Peter Hanstein, 1938).

7. Jean Leclercq, *Aspects of Monasticism*, trans. Mary Dodd, Cistercian Studies Series 7 (Kalamazoo, Michigan: Cistercian Publications, Inc., 1978), 72.

8. Gryson, *The Ministry of Women in the Early Church*, 13; also Aimé Georges Martimort, *Les Diaconesses*, Bibliotheca Ephemerides Liturgicae Subsidia 24 (Rome: Edizioni Liturgiche, 1982), 22–24.

9. See, for example, Clement of Rome's Epistle to the Corinthians 1:38 (Lightfoot 1.2:116–17); Ignatius of Antioch's letter to Polycarp 5 (Lightfoot 2.2:814); and Justin Martyr's first Apology 15 (FP 2:27–28); also, Johannes Schneider, "eunouchos," *Theological Dictionary of the New Testament*, ed. Gerhard Kittel, 2:767–68.

10. John Bugge, *Virginitas: An Essay in the History of a Medieval Ideal*, International Archives of the History of Ideas, series minor 17 (The Hague: Martinus Nijhoff, 1975), 69.

11. As a corrective to a male-centered narration of this early history, see Sandra Schneiders' useful "Reflections on the History of Religious Life," *Turning Points in Religious Life*, ed. Carol Quigley (Wilmington, Delaware: Michael Glazier, 1987), especially 20–22.

12. See, for example, Robert Murray, "The Exhortation to Candidates for ascetical vows at Baptism in the Ancient Syriac Church," *New Testament Studies* 21 (1974), 59–80.

13. See the fine summary on "The Origins of Monasticism in the Eastern Church," in The Rule of St. Benedict, ed. Timothy Fry (Collegeville: Liturgical Press, 1980), 3–41.

14. See Hubert Jedin and John Dolan, eds., *History of the Church*, Vol. 2: *The Imperial Church from Constantine to the Early Middle Ages* (New York: Seabury Press, 1980), 337–42.

15. Edward E. Malone, "Martyrdom and Monastic Profession as a Second Baptism," *Vom Christlichen Mysterium*, eds. Anton Mayer, Johannes Quasten, Burkhard Neunheuser (Düsseldorf: Patmos, 1951), 117–18.

16. Edward E. Malone, *The Monk and the Martyr: The Monk as the Successor of the Martyr*, The Catholic University of America Studies in Christian Antiquity 12 (Washington, D.C.: The Catholic University of America Press, 1950); also, Jean Leclercq, *The Life of Perfection*, trans. Leonard Doyle (Collegeville: The Liturgical Press, 1960), 91–117.

17. Leclercq, *Aspects of Monasticism*, 80.

18. Malone, *The Monk and the Martyr*, 122.

19. Athanasius, *The Life of Antony*, trans. and intr. Robert Gregg (New York: Paulist, 1980), n. 65, 79.

20. Not only did cenobitic monasticism prevail but male cenobitic monasticism began to dominate all forms of religious life. As Sandra Schneiders notes, "Until the 12th century the only forms of feminine religious life known in the West were those which followed the Augustinian Rule and those which followed the Benedictine Rule." Schneiders, "Reflections on the History of Religious Life and Contemporary Development," 27.

21. Jaroslav Pelikan, *Jesus through the Centuries* (New York: Harper & Row, 1985), 114.

22. John Lozano, *Discipleship: Toward an Understanding of Religious Life*, trans. Beatrice Wilczynski (Chicago: Claretian Publications, 1986), 24.

23. *Epistola* 39:3–4 (CSEL 54:299); also, *Epistola* 130:7–14 (CSEL 56:186).

24. *The Ecclesiastical Hierarchy* 6:3, in *Pseudo-Dionysius: The Complete Works*, trans. Colum Luibheid (New York: Paulist Press, 1987), 244.

25. He speaks of the *"musterion monachikes teleioseos"* in *The Ecclesiastical Hierarchy* 6:3 (PG 3:533).

26. Bernhard Poschmann, *Penance and the Anointing of the Sick*, trans. and rev. Francis Courtney (New York: Herder and Herder, 1964), 113–15.

27. Fry, *The Rule of St. Benedict*, 441.

28. Sandra Schneiders, *New Wineskins* (New York: Paulist Press, 1986), 47.

29. Lozano, *Discipleship*, 261.

30. Malone, "Martyrdom and Monastic Profession," 121.

31. Pierre Raffin suggests that it is probably with Shenoudi, a successor of Pachomius (d. 346), that the first formula of profession appeared. Pierre Raffin "Liturgie de l'engagement religieux," *La Maison-Dieu* 104 (1970), 154.

32. Leclercq, *Aspects of Monasticism*, 78.

33. Lozano, *Discipleship*, 268.

34. Richard Yeo, *The Structure and Content of Monastic Profession*, Studia Anselmiana 83 (Rome: Pontificio Ateneo s. Anselmo, 1982), 346.

35. See Ambrose, *De Virginibus* 3.1 (PL 16:231); also *"Ad Virgines Sacras,"* in *Sacramentarium Veronense*, ed. L. C. Mohlberg, Rerum Ecclesiasticarum Documenta, Series Maior Fontes 1 (Rome: Herder, 1966), nn. 1103–4.

36. It is especially René Metz who holds that the marriage rite is the source of the giving of the veil, the offering of a blessing, etc. See his "La nouveau rituel de consécration des vierges sa place dans l'histoire," *La Maison-Dieu* 110 (1972) 105–7. On the nonsacramental status of marriage at this time, see Kenneth Stevenson, *Nuptual Blessing*, Alcuin Club (London: SPCK, 1982), 20–21.

37. René Metz, "Benedictio sive consecratio virginum," *Ephemerides Liturgicae* 80 (1966), 265–93.

38. René Metz, *La consécration des vierges dans l'Eglise romaine* (Paris: Presses Universitaires de France, 1954), 93.

39. Metz, *La consécration des vierges dans l'Eglise romaine*, 88.

40. Odo Casel, "Die Mönchsweihe bei St. Benedikt," *Jahrbuch für Liturgiewissenschaft* 5 (1925), 1–45.

41. Pelikan, *Jesus through the Centuries*, 114.

42. Francois Vandenbroucke, "La Profession, second baptême," *La vie spirituelle* 76 (1947), 255.

43. See, for example, *The Penitential of Theodore* X.1-2 in *Medieval Handbooks of Penance*, trans. John T. McNeill and Helena M. Gamer,

Records of Civilization: Sources and Studies 29 (New York: Octagon Books, Inc., 1965; 1938), 193–94.

44. See André Vauchez, *La spiritualité du moyen âge occidental*, Collection SUP (Paris: Presses Universitaires de France, 1975), 43–45.

45. *Epistola* 165 (PG 99:1524).

46. Jean Leclercq, *The Loving of Learning and the Desire for God*, trans. Catharine Misrahi (New York: Fordham University Press, 1961), chapter 4.

47. Vauchez, *La spiritualité du moyen âge occidental*, 44.

48. Francois Vandenbroucke, *Why Monks?*, Cistercian Studies Series 17 (Washington, D.C.: Cistercian Publications, 1972), 61.

49. Vandenbroucke, *Why Monks?*, 85.

50. *Ecclesiastical Hierarchies* 5.3 (Luibheid, 237); 6.3 (Luibheid, 244–45).

51. *Apologeticus ad Hugonem et Rodbertum reges Francorum* PL 139:463.

52. Pelikan, *Jesus through the Centuries*, 117.

53. Angelus Haussling, *Mönchskonvent und Eucharistiefeier*, *Liturgiewissenschaftliche Quellen und Forschungen* 58 (Münster: Aschendorff, 1973), 156.

54. Casel, "Die Mönchsweihe," 29.

55. See, for example, the comparison between Cyril's *Mystagogical Catechesis* and the ritual in *The Initiation of Monks* outlined in Malone, *The Monk and the Martyr*, 125–27.

56. Casel, "Die Mönchsweihe," 34.

57. Vandenbroucke, *Why Monks?*, 103.

58. For a further discussion of this development, see pages 39–41.

59. Vauchez, *La spiritualité du moyen âge occidental*, 98; for a further discussion of their spirituality, see Caroline Walker Bynum, "The Spirituality of the Regular Canons in the Twelfth Century," *Jesus as Mother: Studies in the Spirituality of the High Middle Ages* (Berkeley: University of California Press, 1982), 22–58.

60. Vandenbroucke, *Why Monks?*, 88.

61. *Clementianarum* 3.10.8, in *Decretales Gregorii Papae IX*, Corpus Juris Canonici 2 (Cologne, 1779), 364.

62. This rule is actually two rules, *Regula Secunda* (PL 32:1449–52) and *Regula ad servos Dei* (PL 32:1377–84), which were shaped according to the ideas found in Augustine's letter 211 (PL 33:958–65) addressed to nuns.

63. For example, Hilda of Whitby (+680) whom Bede memorializes in his *Historia Ecclesiastica Gentis Anglorum* 4.23 (PL 95:208–12). For an introduction to the influence of women religious in religious life of the Middle Ages, see R. W. Southern, *Western Society and the Church in the*

Middle Ages, The Pelican History of the Church 2 (Harmondsworth, England: Penguin, 1970), 309–18

64. One exception was the Order of Fontevrault, founded by Robert of Arbrissel (d. 1117), which was governed throughout its history by an Abbess General. See René Niderst, *Robert d'Arbrissel et les origines de l'ordre de Fontevrault* (Rodez: G. Subervie, 1952).

65. "Each and every nun, both at the present time and in the future, in whatsoever . . . order they may belong, or in whatever part of the world they may be, must henceforth remain in their monastery within a perpetual enclosure." *Liber Sextus*, 3:16, Corpus Juris Canonici 2, 324.

66. Schneiders, "Reflections on the History of Religious Life and Contemporary Development," 31. Schneiders further comments that the choice of some women to live as third-order members instead of cloistered second-order religious "represents the first successful feminine out-maneuvering of male restrictions for the sake of apostolic involvement."

67. See E. W. McDonnell, *The Beguines and Beghards in Medieval Culture* (New Brunswick: Rutgers University Press, 1954).

68. Jean Becquet, "Etienne de Muret," *Dictionnaire de Spiritualité*, 4:1504–1514.

69. T. P. Van Zijl, *Gerard Groote: Ascetic and Reformer 1340-1384*, CUA Studies in Mediaeval History NS 18 (Washington, D.C.: Catholic University of America, 1963).

70. See Stevenson, *We Join Together: The Rite of Marriage*, 50–52.

71. Vauchez, *Why Monks?*, 144.

72. "It was in the twelfth century when the Augustinians . . . began elaborating the monastic vow into the three vows of poverty, chastity and obedience. Later, in 1202, Pope Innocent III, in a letter to a monk of Subiaco, mentioned the three vows, the first time they appear in an official document." Leonardo Boff, *God's Witnesses in the Heart of the World*, trans. and ed. Robert Fath (Chicago: Claret Center for Resources in Spirituality, 1981).

73. Session 25, 3–4 December 1563, "De regularibus et monialibus," chapters 5, 7, 21, 10 and 15, respectively.

74. Iriarte, *Franciscan History*, 195–225.

75. Gabriel de Sainte-Marie-Magdaleine, "Carmes Déchaussés," *Dictionnaire de Spiritualité*, 2:171–209.

76. Jules Baudot, "Mauristes," *Dictionnaire de Théologie Catholique*, 10:405–43.

77. Heimbucher, *Die Orden und Kongregationen der katholischen Kirche*, 1:363–373.

78. See the summary in Wolfgang Frey, *The Act of Religious Profession*, The Catholic University of America Canon Law Series 63 (Washington, D.C.: The Catholic University of America Press, 1931), 31–32.

79. *Liber Sextus* 3.15, Corpus Juris Canonici 2, 323–24.

80. See Joseph de Guibert, *The Jesuits: Their Spiritual Doctrine and Practice*, trans. William Young (Chicago: Institute of Jesuit Sources, 1964), 139–51; also, James Brodrick, *The Origin of the Jesuits* (Westport: Greenwood, 1971 [1940]).

81. Vincent de Paul (d. 1660), founder of the Sisters of Charity, once wrote to his sisters, "If ever there should appear in your midst some fool who says 'We should be religious, it would be far better . . . the company would then be ready to receive extreme unction. . . . For whoever says 'religious' says 'cloistered' and the Daughters of Charity must be able to go anywhere." *Saint Vincent De Paul: correspondance, entretiens, documents*, ed. Pierre Coste, 14 vols. (Paris, 1920–1925), 10:658.

82. Heimbucher, *Die Orden und Kongregationen der katholischen Kirche*, 1:628–39; also, Teresa Ledóchowska, *Angela Merici and the Company of St. Ursula*, trans. Mary Teresa Neyland (Rome: Ancora, 1968).

83. Heimbucher, *Die Orden und Kongregationen der katholischen Kirche*, 1:641–46.

84. *Saint Vincent de Paul*, 1:25: "There is no further trace of perpetual vows after the death of Saint Vincent and . . . in 1718 the practice of taking annual vows had become universally established." Pierre Coste, *The Life and Works of St. Vincent De Paul*, trans. Joseph Leonard, 3 vols. (Westminster: Newman Press, 1952), 1:349.

85. On the progressive recognition of such communities by Rome, see Donnell Anthony Walsh, *The New Law on Secular Institutes*, The Catholic University of America Canon Law Studies 347 (Washington, D.C.: Catholic University of America Press, 1953), 28–36.

86. *Codicis Iuris Canonici Fontes*, Peter Gaspari, ed., 9 vols. (Rome: Typis polyglottis Vaticanis, 1923–39), 3:563–566 (n. 644).

87. Canons 487 and 488.

88. See the partial enumeration of such communities in Heimbucher, *Die Orden und Kongregationen der katholischen Kirche*, 2:341–551.

89. See Bernard Ristuccia, *Quasi-Religious Societies*, The Catholic University of America Canon Law Studies 261 (Washington, D.C.: Catholic University of America Press, 1949), especially 13–44.

90. Pius XII (d. 1958) officially established secular institutes in 1947, with his apostolic constitution *Provida Mater Ecclesia*, Acta Apostolicae Sedis 39 (1947), 119.

91. Schneiders, "Reflections on the History of Religious Life and Contemporary Development," 35–36.

The Theological Context

The Emerging Sacramental Framework

As our historical survey has indicated, the relationship between baptism and religious profession is an evolving one; it has assumed radically divergent emphases throughout its history. In the beginning, though the community may have lacked refined theological language or a systematic framework for articulating its belief, baptism and eucharist were foundational to establishing and identifying the Christian community. Consequently, the early community knew no substitute for baptism, which was a decisive act of reconciliation, initiation into the death and resurrection of Jesus, the invitation into the eschatological banquet and the point of entry into the community of the elect.

The determinative nature of baptism seems to have been especially well emphasized by the followers of Pachomius (d. 346), whose own vocation was intimately connected with his baptism. In the Pachomian community, unbaptized candidates were admitted into the brotherhood, but their initial period of integration into the community was also the time of their catechumenate. These monk-catechumens were baptized at the annual Easter reunion of all the members of the community. Thus, for some monks, "baptism was quite closely connected with their vocation and their concept of monks."[1]

With the decline of adult baptism and the growing influence of monasticism in the life of the church, religious profession slowly acquired more of a sacramental profile and simultaneously asserted its independence from baptism. Increasingly described in sacramental language, profession was considered a means for forgiving sin and was believed by some to be superior to ordination and even baptism. It is possible to suggest that—especially in the early Middle Ages—monastic profession replaced baptism as the normative adult ritual for initiation into a life of holiness. In effect, it became the true sacrament of initiation to the full Christian life.

Various developments in sacramental thought and language in the 12th and 13th centuries, however, eventually excluded religious profession from the church's list of official sacraments. Until this time, sacrament *(sacramentum* or *musterion)* was a rather elusive concept, easily predicated of a wide range of ecclesial acts and artifacts.[2] Throughout the patristic and much of the medieval period, this concept retained its elasticity. Thus, Ambrose (d. 397) could refer to the washing of the feet as a sacrament,[3] and Augustine (d. 430) could generously apply the term to various catechumenal rites, feasts of the church, devotional practices and prayers.[4] Pseudo-Dionysius (flourished around 500) considered the consecration of an altar a sacrament,[5] Peter Damian (d. 1072) listed the anointing of a king among the sacraments,[6] and Hugh of St. Victor (d. 1142) identified a whole category of sacraments that were not necessary for salvation but aids to grace *(sacramenta ad excercitationem),* such as holy water.[7] Fulbert of Chartres (d. 1028) taught that there were only two sacraments, while Bernard of Clairvaux (d. 1153) could speak of ten, twelve or even more sacraments.[8]

Though he did not originate the sevenfold schema,[9] it is undoubtedly the formulation of Peter Lombard (d. 1160) that became determinative for setting the number of official sacraments at seven. This formulation, contained in his *Sentences,* was reflected in the profession of faith outlined by Innocent III in a letter of 1208,[10] was officially reiterated by the church at the Second Council of Lyons (1274)[11] and in the *Decree for the Armenians* from the Council of Florence (1439),[12] and was definitively confirmed at the Council of Trent (1547).[13] The progressive acceptance of this formulation effectively removed religious profession from the church's list of sacraments.

Religious Profession as Sacramental or Sacrament?

Peter Lombard also seems to have originated the term "sacramental" *(sacramentalia),* which he used when referring to certain baptismal rituals, such as exorcisms, that were considered of secondary importance.[14] This concept found a parallel in the work of Hugh of St. Victor who distinguished between sacraments that were necessary for salvation *(sacramenta ad salutem),* sacraments that were not necessary for salvation but contributed to our sanctification *(sacramenta ad exercitationem),* and sacraments that prepared for the celebration of other sacraments *(sacramenta ad praeparationem).*[15] Baptism was included in the first group, the distribution of ashes in the second and the consecration of a church in the third. Various canonists of the 12th and 13th centuries, such as Rufinus (flourished around 1157) and Simon of Tournai (flourished around 1190) also employed a fourfold division of the sacraments that distinguished between sacraments necessary for salvation *(sacramenta salutaria),* sacraments such as matins and lauds that occurred in the celebration of the Offices *(sacramenta ministratoria),* sacraments that venerated the memory of a holy mystery such as Christmas *(sacramenta veneratoria)* and sacraments that prepared for the celebration of other sacraments *(sacramenta praeparatoria).*[16] Eventually, however, all of those rites not thought to convey sanctifying grace were no longer called sacraments, a term now officially reserved for only seven rites of the church. The others were called sacramentals. As defined in the 1917 Code of Canon Law, sacramentals were all those "things or actions which the church regularly uses, by way of a sort of imitation of the sacraments to obtain by her prayers effects especially of a spiritual nature."[17]

This is how religious profession is understood in the writings of Thomas Aquinas (d. 1274). Like many of his contemporaries, he did not count it among the official sacraments. Thomas did not classify religious profession as a sacrament because he did not believe that this or any other sacramental was a source of sanctifying grace *ex opere operato.*[18] On the other hand, Thomas did believe that every sacramental had certain effects upon those who willingly engaged in such rites. The specific effect of religious profession in the view of Thomas was the remission of all sins.[19]

The theological opinion reflected in the work of Thomas Aquinas achieved universal acceptance in the late Middle Ages and until our own day it has been customary to refer to religious profession as a sacramental and sometimes specifically as a "baptismal sacramental."[20] Without denying the validity of this formulation—which happily finds a baptismal referent in the very origin of the term "sacramental"—one yet wonders whether our contemporary understanding of religious profession is sufficiently served by this concept of "sacramental."

In some respects, the current situation in sacramental theology is akin to that which prevailed before the work of Lombard, when the church did not limit itself to a vocabulary of seven sacraments. In the tradition of Augustine, Pseudo-Dionysius and Hugh of St. Victor, scholars such as Semmelroth, Schillebeeckx and Rahner have begun again to expand our sacramental horizons. They and many of their contemporaries have helped us to understand that Christ is the primordial sacrament and that the church is the abiding presence of that primordial sacrament in the world and is the source of all other sacraments.[21] Such formulations have worked their way into the mainstream of Roman Catholic thought and are embedded in the documents of the Second Vatican Council. The Council taught that the church is the sacrament of Christ who in turn is the source of every sacrament.[22]

In this broadening theological context, it seems beneficial to consider religious life and religious profession not so much as *a* sacramental but rather *as* sacramental. A significant number of authors since the Second Vatican Council have suggested in one way or another that religious life can or should be understood as a sacrament.[23] Few such writers have taken seriously the rites of religious profession in their attempts to promote the sacramental nature of religious life and fewer still would admit that the profession rite itself is a sacrament in the narrow sense of that term. Yet the church's liturgy is an authentic source of teaching, an expression of what could be called the church's first theology.[24] Consequently, the rites of initiation into religious life need to be an essential focus for any reflection on the sacramentality of religious life and religious profession.

Sacramental Insights from Karl Rahner

In attempting to define the nature of a sacrament for today, Rahner readily admits that even though every conferral and acceptance of grace in the church has a "quasi-sacramental structure," these do not exist in every case as a sacrament in the technical sense of that term.[25] According to Rahner, sacrament in the strict sense occurs

> when the church in her official, organized, public capacity precisely as the source of redemptive grace meets the individual in the actual ultimate accomplishment of her nature . . . [which] bring[s] into activity the very essence of the church herself.[26]

He further asserts:

> A fundamental act of the church in an individual's regard, in situations that are decisive for the individual, an act which truly involves the nature of the church as the historical, eschatological presence of redemptive grace, is *ipso facto* a sacrament, even if it were only later that reflection was directed to its sacramental character that follows from its connection with the nature of the church.[27]

Finally, Rahner insists on the unconditional engagement of the individual and of the church in any truly sacramental act.

> It must be possible for her prayer to be offered here as a manifestation of the unconditional promise of salvation for the whole life of a person such as is at stake in this situation, and as a prayer that is certainly heard, because it is truly and indubitably a prayer of the church. It must unconditionally engage the responsibility of the church, it must radically bring into action the church inasmuch as she is the fundamental sacrament of grace for the individual, as such, in critical situations, for the purpose of conferring grace on that individual. Therefore, it is an *opus operatum* with grace as its effect. In other words, it is a sacrament.[28]

To discover whether or not religious life, confirmed through religious profession,[29] could be considered a sacrament within this framework, it seems necessary to determine whether it meets the following criteria: 1) Does it involve the church on the level of the church's true nature? 2) Does it authentically presume the church's promise of redemptive grace? 3) Does it decisively engage the individual with the unconditional offer of salvation? Though it might be possible to answer these questions according to the opinion of various theologians, like Rahner himself, the principle that the church's worship embodies its truest belief suggests that we first discover whether the rites themselves offer answers to these questions. We will briefly consider such questions, therefore, in light of the Rite of Religious Profession,[30] with specific reference to the Roman Franciscan Rite of Religious Profession.[31] This information will then be supplemented by the relevant teachings from the documents of the Second Vatican Council and the writings of Rahner.

Celebrating the True Nature of the Church

Beginning with the first question concerning the involvement of the church on the level of its true nature, the introduction to the rite first reminds us that it is none other than the church itself that receives the vows of those who make profession.[32] Furthermore, by the very fact that the rites presume that religious profession occurs within the context of eucharist,[33] which the Constitution on the Sacred Liturgy considers the font and summit of the church's life,[34] the rite implicitly attests to the fact that profession is an essentially ecclesial act. More specifically, in the ritual request, the examination and the solemn blessing,[35] it is clear that profession is an official invitation and acceptance of the church's mission to live the gospel in service to others in such a way that it will "build up the church, advance the salvation of the world, and be a convincing sign of the blessings of the world to come."[36]

The ecclesial nature of religious profession is also underscored in the Dogmatic Constitution on the Church, which notes that: "The state of life . . . which is constituted by the profession of the evangelical counsels, while not entering into the hierarchical structure of the church, belongs undeniably to her life and holiness."[37] The Council could assert that perpetual profession, in which one pledges oneself to the practice of the counsels, shows forth "the unbreakable bond of union that exists between Christ and his bride the church."[38] Rahner, as well, believes that the vows of poverty, chastity and obedience have a special status in the church and that "in virtue of this fact they have an *essential function* to perform in the church prior to any question of the 'useful works' which the orders perform on the church's behalf." They belong "to the essence of the church."[39] In another place, speaking of monastic profession, Rahner remarks:

Something is not only happening between God and humankind, but as the center and the mediator which alone vouchsafes a true immediacy, the church is present at this hour. She becomes tangible and concrete in the hierarchically structured community of an abbey. Here the church becomes event.[40]

Thus, from the viewpoint of the rites, the official teaching of the church and the theological reflections of Rahner, it seems possible to hold that religious profession authentically engages the church as church in its truest nature.

The Celebration of Redemptive Grace

As to the more difficult question of whether or not religious profession authentically presumes the church's promise of redemptive grace, we again turn to the rites of religious profession to begin our search for an answer. What is initially most striking in this regard is the number of times that God's help or grace is presumed for the fulfillment of the vows that are being professed. For example, during the examination before the profession, the candidates are asked: "Are you resolved, with the help of God *(Dei adiuvante gratia),* to undertake that life of perfect chastity, obedience, and poverty, . . ." and again: "Are you resolved, with the help of the Holy Spirit *(Sancti Spiritus subveniente munere),* to spend your whole life in the generous service. . . ."[41] Perhaps most dramatic is the formula for religious profession, one adaptation of which has the candidates asserting, "Since for the glory of God, the Lord has given me this grace of living more perfectly and with firm will the gospel of Jesus Christ. . . ."[42] This surety of grace is echoed in the proper *Hanc igitur* proposed for insertion in Eucharistic Prayer I on the day of profession, which proclaims, "By your grace they have dedicated their lives to you today."[43]

Furthermore, the rite continuously petitions for such grace on behalf of those being professed. The litany of all saints, for example, includes the petition: "Give these servants of yours the grace of perseverance."[44] The closing prayer after the litany petitions: "By the grace of the Holy Spirit, purify them from all sin and set them on fire with your love."[45] The solemn blessing or consecration, as well, prays, "Send them the spirit of holiness; help them to fulfill in faith what you have enabled them to promise in joy."[46] Likewise, the final blessing prays, "May he protect you always by his grace so that you may fulfill the duties of your vocation with a faithful heart."[47] This image is further reflected in the prayer after communion: "Increase in them the fire of your Holy Spirit."[48]

Finally, we recall that the rite of religious profession presumably takes place within the context of the eucharist, the church's prized celebration of redemptive grace in Christ. Furthermore, the ritual continuously parallels the act of eucharistic thanksgiving and the act of religious profession. This is demonstrated not only by the interplay of rites and texts, but in a special way by the insertion of the previously noted petitions at the very heart of the eucharist. The parallel between profession and eucharist is well summarized in the alternate prayer after communion that proclaims:

> Lord, may the reception of this sacrament, and the solemnizing of this profession bring us joy. Let this *twofold act of devotion* help your servants to serve the church and humankind in the spirit of your love.[49] [Emphasis added.]

Reflecting on the nature of monastic profession, Rahner remarks: "The church not only supports this event approvingly and protectingly, but she herself becomes an event in it." He continues:

> But when one asks: Where then is the church, where does the church become event, a holy convocation of people to divine grace, which redeems and blesses with God himself, and to the fellowship of humankind in God? In the ultimate and truest sense we need not answer: Where laws are enacted and church policy is made. Instead, we must say: There where faith, hope and love happen, there where life is consecrated to the accomplishment of the eternal eucharist and is dedicated to the eternal God. Therein does the church become event. Therefore the church grows in this hour; therefore does she, in such an event,

appear in her truest essence, which is the apportionment of the world which God himself brings tangibly into being through his grace in the freedom of the infinite Spirit.[50]

It seems possible in this perspective to suggest that the act of religious profession is more than the recalling of baptismal grace and more than the evocation of personal grace *(ex opere operantis).* Rather, in the context of this fundamentally ecclesial event, it seems that true redemptive grace is imparted and accepted through the act of profession.

Celebrating the Unconditional Offer of Salvation

Finally, in light of Rahner's definition of sacrament, does profession decisively engage the individual with the unconditional offer of salvation? The introduction to the Rite of Perpetual Profession during Mass recognizes that in this ritual "a religious binds [himself/herself] to God forever."[51] As previously noted, the church itself initiates the call of the candidates to this relationship,[52] and in response to this call the candidates ask that they "may persevere until death in the Lord's service and in . . . [this] religious community," to which the community responds, "Thanks be to God."[53] Finally, regarding this call, the introduction to the litany notes that it is truly God who has called these candidates "to follow Christ in the religious life," and thus it is not only the blessing of the church and the support of the community which is invoked, but the very grace of God.[54]

Besides the various parts of the ritual which acknowledge that religious profession is a response to a call from God, we note that the local community and the whole church pray that the candidates will persevere in this life until its fulfillment in heaven. At the end of the examination, the presider "confirms the intention of those to be professed" by praying: "May God who has begun the good work in you bring it to fulfillment before the day of Christ Jesus."[55] Even more dramatic and definitive than the confirmation of intentions or the prayers for perseverance is the stark assurance of salvation as announced by the one who accepts the vows. For example, in the Roman-Franciscan Ritual, after accepting the vows "in the name of the church," the presider adds, "And on the part of almighty God, if you observe them, I promise you life everlasting."[56]

The bold articulation of this promised effect, of course, does not imply that every perpetually professed religious automatically reaches this goal—just as ecclesial initiation does not ensure that the promise of the sacrament is always fulfilled. In this and every instance of a gracious invitation from God, a free and continuous response from the individual needs to be forthcoming, and a willingness to cooperate with the grace of this encounter with God is essential for the effectiveness of the profession. What seems clear is that aside from the manner or degree of response that the candidate makes to this promise, the specific purpose of religious profession and the whole of the vowed life, is to engage one in the imitation of Christ and union with God.[57] This engagement begins with a call from God, who is the source of every call. To be sure, this is not the first time such an unconditional offer of salvation has been given, for the foundational salvific call from God is unquestionably confirmed in baptism. The fact that an unconditional call was once given, however, does not negate the fact that this call can be sounded again in a new and special way through religious profession. This renewed invitation demonstrates—some would say in the most perfect way—that we are reaching for a goal that lies beyond this present world, union with God.[58]

Though we have employed a theological framework provided by Karl Rahner to explore the sacramental character of religious profession, Rahner himself is very cautious about calling profession a sacrament. Thus, in the introduction to *Meditations on the Sacraments*, he comments:

> I have included a sermon given at a religious profession because it seems to have the same basic theme as the meditations on marriage and priesthood, which are sacraments of one's "state in life." In doing so I am not, of course, asserting that religious profession is a sacrament.[59]

On the other hand, Rahner does not deny that it is a sacrament and seems to offer strong support for the sacramentality of religious profession. He declares that, in religious profession,

> the church marks another grace-filled realization of one of the hallmarks of her own reality. All of this points at its deepest level to God: to him who accepts this life, who blesses the site of his veneration, who makes the church grow and who reveals himself in all the glory of his own life, which is eternal love.[60]

It would be difficult not to admit as sacramental any event in which the church marks a "grace-filled realization of one of the hallmarks of her own reality."

The Value of the Sacramentality of Profession

Asserting the sacramentality of religious profession admittedly raises questions. Two of the most important are the relationship of profession to the other "seven" and the advantage of presenting profession in a sacramental framework.

The Relationship of Profession to the Other Sacraments

Throughout the history of the church the sacraments have never been considered equal to each other in dignity or ecclesial import. Rather, baptism and eucharist have enjoyed a marked priority in our sacramental system.

Beginning with the clear New Testament witness to these sacraments, there has been consistent evidence of baptism and eucharist in virtually every community that has called itself Christian from the primitive age until our own time. At every stage of the church's development, baptism and eucharist have always been considered sacraments,[61] and were the first such rites to be called *sacramentum* by Tertullian.[62] Besides this historical precedence, these two sacraments also enjoy a clear theological priority; in the Middle Ages they are distinguished as the sacraments necessary for salvation.[63] The Council of

Trent (1545–1563) taught that all the sacraments are not of equal dignity,[64] considered the eucharist the most excellent of the sacraments[65] and called baptism the sacrament of faith "without which no one was ever justified."[66] This continues to be the view of the contemporary church that calls baptism the "door to life,"[67] considers eucharist the most excellent of all sacraments[68] and teaches that together baptism and eucharist have a special place in the church's worship.[69] Rahner himself cautions:

> It would be possible to think of and construct other such acts, and so deduce more than seven sacraments . . . [and] then show in all probability that these imagined additional acts in which the essence of the church found expression cannot really be unmistakably proved to be of equal rank with the seven sacraments that do exist.[70]

To recognize that religious profession is not equal in rank with baptism and eucharist is not to disprove its sacramental character. Profession finds a clearer sacramental parallel in other "secondary" sacraments of one's "state in life," such as marriage and priesthood.

The Value of a Sacramental Framework for Profession

Our intention in asserting the sacramental nature of profession is not for the sake of demonstrating the superiority of religious profession over some other sacramental action, nor is it an attempt to revive a medieval belief in the superiority of religious life over that of any other state in the church. Rather, the projection of a sacramental framework can be helpful in defining and understanding this charism in the contemporary church. Through such definition and understanding, "in fidelity to a concrete vocation, to a mission, to the charism of an order or congregation, we reveal our fidelity to the absolute vocation,"[71] union with God in Christ. The paths to such union are manifold, yet through the centuries the church has underscored certain of these as especially illustrative of and effective for achieving this goal. Acknowledging the sacramentality of religious life achieved through religious profession is, therefore, similar to recognizing the sacramentality of the married state achieved through the exchange of vows: Each in a unique way reflects and achieves the union with God in Christ to which we are summoned in baptism.

Furthermore, an awareness of the sacramental nature of religious profession suggests specific and important consequences both for the formation of religious candidates and also for the celebration of these initiatory rites.[72] Profession and religious life as sacrament presume that, as with every sacrament, these are christic, ecclesial and individual events. Consequently, candidates for full initiation into religious life need to develop clear images of these aspects of their vocation and to be led to ritualize them with integrity.

Finally, underscoring the sacramental character of profession immerses the religious in a "sacramental world," where they will hopefully be more apt to recognize that "sanctifying grace is found everywhere . . . [and] the world is permanently graced at its root."[73] Such insight might encourage religious to acknowledge more readily and so support the sacramentality of other Christian life-styles. They would encourage all to respond more completely to the call of holiness extended to every baptized person.

Summary

Although according to a strictly post-Lombardian, scholastic framework it would be difficult to define religious profession as a sacrament, we have other perspectives that allow for the sacramentality of this ecclesial act. At a time when the church had a broader concept of sacramentality, religious life or religious profession could be considered a sacrament in the East and West by such diverse representatives as Augustine,[74] Pseudo-Dionysius,[75] Theodore the Studite (d. 826),[76] Peter Damian,[77]

Hugh of St. Victor,[78] Sicard of Cremona (d. 1215),[79] the Monk Job (flourished around 1270),[80] Simeon of Thessalonica (d. 1429),[81] and a vast array of other spiritual writers, canonists and theologians who sought to explain its special charism in sacramental terms.[82]

In our own day we have witnessed an important expansion of the concept of sacramentality akin to that which existed before those 12th-century developments that eventually led to the distinction between sacrament and sacramental. Through the work of theologians such as Edward Schillebeeckx we are coming to understand that sacraments are defined by the person of Jesus, embodied in and mediated by the church. More specifically, Schillebeeckx has helped us to understand sacraments as "ecclesial acts of worship, in which the church in communion of grace with its heavenly head (i.e., together with Christ), pleads with the Father for the bestowal of grace on the recipient of the sacrament, and in which at the same time the church itself, as saving community in holy union with Christ, performs a saving act."[83]

Such a perspective, though particular in its contribution, is yet characteristic of a general approach in contemporary sacramentality that begins in Christ and extends through the church's life and action. Rahner, as well, presents a broad understanding of sacrament that begins in Christ, extends through the church and finds particular focus in those ecclesial acts that reveal the true nature of the church, are the source of redemptive grace and offer an unconditional promise of salvation for the whole life of the individual. In this perspective, religious profession and therefore religious life is clearly sacramental.

Beyond the work of individual theologians, the very worship of the church, which provides the context for religious profession, seems to point to its sacramental character. If one respects the church's worship as the embodiment of our most authentic belief, it becomes difficult to deny that the profession liturgy is sacramental, for it ritually presumes and promises the gracious action of God and the full endorsement of the universal church.

This is especially true of the "Rite of Religious Profession of Men." As indicated throughout this chapter, however, there are sometimes significant differences between this rite and the "Rite of Religious Profession of Women."[84] The former is more prone to employ language that emphasizes the ministerial, active and ecclesial nature of religious life, while the latter tends to emphasize the exemplary, receptive and nonhierarchical nature of religious life.[85] This disparity is an unfortunate reflection of the church's past tendency to restrict religious women to a cloistered, exemplary life, receptive to the rules and directions of male ecclesiastics. When women attempted to move outside the cloister, especially after the Council of Trent, ecclesial recognition was sometimes only grudgingly given. Aside from disturbing evocation of this oppressive history, the disparity between these two rites is also troublesome because it is thereby easier to demonstrate the sacramentality of religious profession for men than for women. On the other hand, the essential nature of religious life—reflected in both rituals—demands comparable conclusions. Therefore, we believe that the rites of religious profession for women and men, in their texts, ritual actions and intention, demonstrate the sacramental nature of religious profession and consequently the sacramental nature of religious life.

To hold for the sacramentality of religious profession does not imply the displacement or overshadowing of the other traditionally defined sacraments of the church. The value of so defining profession is threefold. First, it contributes to the ongoing definition of religious life for today, especially in view of our contemporary understanding of sacrament. Second, it informs and enriches both the personal and the ritual formation of candidates for initiation into religious life. Finally, it encourages religious to acknowledge the sacramentality of the world in which they have been called to witness and serve, and by consequence encourages other believers to admit the sacramentality of their own vocation. In our view it is not only defensible but also enriching to consider religious profession and therefore religious life at least sacramental, if not a sacrament.

Notes

1. Leclercq, *Aspects of Monasticism*, 77; see the pertinent texts in Armand Veilleux, *La liturgie dans le cénobitisme pachômien au quatrième siècle*, Studia Anselmiana 57 (Rome: Herder, 1968), 198–206.

2. For a thorough treatment of the development of this concept, see Josef Finkenzeller, *Die Lehre von den Sakramenten im allgemeinen von der Schrift bis zur Scholastik*, Handbuch der Dogmengeschichte, Band IV, Fasz. 1a (Freiburg im Br.: Herder, 1980).

3. *De Mysteriis* 6:31–33 (PL 16:416–17).

4. See, for example, *Sermones* 227 (PL 38:1099–1101) and 228.3 (PL 38:1102).

5. *The Ecclesiastical Hierarchy*, 4:12 (Luibheid, 232).

6. *Sermo* 69 (PL 144:899).

7. *De Sacramentis* 1.9.7 (PL 176:327) and 2.9.1 (PL 176:471).

8. See Finkenzeller, *Die Lehre von den Sakramenten*, 72–74, 119–23 and 158–72.

9. "An early catalog of seven sacraments is found in the tract *De sacramentis* of Master Simon. It is almost identical with that of the contemporary, anonymous *Sententiae divinitatis* (around 1145), which is partially dependent on the work of Master Simon." Edward Kilmartin, *Christian Liturgy: Theology and Practice* (Kansas City: Sheed and Ward, 1988), 276.

10. "Eius exemplo," 18 December 1208 (DENZ., n. 424).

11. DENZ., n. 465.

12. "Exultate Deo," 22 November 1439 (DENZ., n. 695).

13. Session VII, 3 March 1547 (DENZ., n. 844).

14. *Sententiae* 4.6.8 (PL 192:855).

15. *De Sacramentis* 1.9.7 (PL 176:327) and 2.9.1 (PL 176:471).

16. The critical texts from these canonists, with commentary, can be found together in J. de Ghellinck, *Le Mouvement théologique du XIIe siècle*,

Museum Lessianum—Section Historique 10 (Brussels: L'Edition Universelle, 1948), 537–47.

17. Canon 1144.

18. *Summa Theologica* i–ii, q. 108, a. 2, ad 2; iii, q. 65, a. 1, ad 3.

19. *Summa Theologica* iia iiae, q. 189, a. 3, ad 3.

20. See, for example, Francois Vandenbroucke, *Why Monks?* Cistercian Studies Series 17, trans. Leon Brockman (Washington, D.C.: Cistercian Publications, 1972), 100; also, Leclercq, *Aspects of Monasticism*, 90–91.

21. See, for example, Otto Semmelroth, *Church and Sacraments* (Notre Dame: Fides, 1965); Edward Schillebeeckx, *Christ the Sacrament of the Encounter with God* (New York: Sheed and Ward, 1963); and Karl Rahner, "The Church and the Sacraments," in his *Inquiries* (New York: Herder and Herder, 1964), 191–299. Some of these assertions were already appearing in the previous century as, for example, in the work of J. A. Moehler and J. H. Oswald who emphasized the sacramentality of the whole church in their *Die dogmatische Lehre von den heiligen Sakramenten der katholischen Kirche*, 2nd ed. (Münster: Aschendorff, 1894), 1:12–13.

22. DCC, nn. 1, 9, 48; also GCD, n. 55 (DOL, n. 1102).

23. Among English writings on the topic are: Joseph Iannone, "Religious Brother: Sacrament of the Church," *Review for Religious* 24 (1965), 606–17; Eric Meyer, "Is Religious Life a Sacrament?" *Review for Religious* 33 (1974), 1100–20; Philip Rosata, "Toward a Sacramental and Social Vision of Religious Life," *Review for Religious* 36 (1977), 501–13; John Rotelle and Edward Manning, "The Fraternity—Sacrament of Love," *Review for Religious* 27 (1968), 393–410; J. M. R. Tillard, "In the Wake of Sacramental Life," *Donum Dei* 4 (1962), 61–81; idem, "Religious Life, Sacrament of God's Power," *Review for Religious* 23 (1964), 420–32; idem, "Religious Life, Sacrament of God's Presence," *Review for Religious* 23 (1964), 6–14.

24. This concept is captured in the liturgical axiom, *"lex orandi, lex credendi,"* attributed to Prosper of Aquitaine (d. around 463) and reiterated, for example, in the *General Instruction of the Roman Missal*, nn. 3 and 10 (DOL, nn. 1378 and 1385). On this topic see, for example, Aidan Kavanagh, *On Liturgical Theology* (New York: Pueblo Publishing Company, 1984), especially 73–95; David Power, *Unsearchable Riches* (New York: Pueblo Publishing Company, 1984), especially 144–71; and Geoffrey Wainwright, *Doxology* (New York: Oxford University Press, 1980), especially 218–83.

25. *Karl Rahner, The Church and the Sacraments*, Quaestiones Disputatae 9, trans. W. J. O'Hara (Freiburg im Br.: Herder, 1963), 22.

26. Rahner, *The Church and the Sacraments*, 22.

27. Rahner, *The Church and the Sacraments*, 41.

28. Rahner, *The Church and the Sacraments*, 68.

29. In this discussion of the sacramentality of religious profession, our focus is perpetual profession that, because of its definitive nature, defines the fullness of religious life and is the end of the initiatory process into a religious community.

30. *Rite of Religious Profession* (Washington, D.C.: The United States Catholic Conference, 1974); hereafter, RRP. See part two of this volume for the complete text.

31. *Roman Franciscan Rite of Religious Profession* (Washington, D.C.: Franciscan Liturgical Projects, 1980); hereafter, RFR.

32. RRP Introduction, n. 2.

33. RRP Introduction, n. 6.

34. CSL, n. 10 (DOL, n. 10).

35. In the Rite of Religious Profession for Men, this is RRP 1:55, RRP 1:57 and RRP 1:67, respectively. In the Rite of Religious Profession for Women, this is RRP 2:60, RRP 2:62 and RRP 2:72.

36. For men, RRP 1:67; for women, the significantly different text is "cherish the church . . . love the whole world . . . teaching all people to look forward in joy and hope to the good things of heaven," RRP 2:72.

For a further examination of the texts of profession in terms of their ecclesial presumption, see I. M. Calabuig, "Note sulla teologia e spiritualità della vita religiosa alla luce dell,' *Ordo Professionis*," in *Per una Presenza Viva Dei Religiosi nella Chiesa e nel Mondo*, ed. A. Favale, 2nd ed. (Turin: Elle Di Ci, 1970), 949–55.

37. DCC, n. 44 (VC II, 405).

38. DCC, n. 44 (VC II, 404).

39. Karl Rahner, "On the Evangelical Counsels," in *Theological Investigations*, Vol. 8: *Further Theology of the Spiritual Life 2*, trans. David Bourke (London: Darton, Longman and Todd, 1971), 163, 165.

40. Karl Rahner, *Meditations on the Sacraments* (New York: Seabury Press, 1977), 102.

41. For men, RRP 1:57; for women, RRP 2:62.

42. RFR, n. 139.

43. For men, RRP 1:73; for women, the significantly different text is "By your grace they join themselves more closely to your Son today," RRP 2:80.

44. For men, RRP 1:62; for women, RRP 2:67.

45. For men, RRP 1:63; for women, RRP 2:68.

46. For men, RRP 1:67; for women, the significantly different text is "send the fire of the Holy Spirit into the hearts of your daughters to keep alive within them the holy desire he has given them," RRP 2:72.

47. For men, RRP 1:76; for women, RRP 2:83.

48. RRP Appendix.

49. RRP Appendix.

50. Rahner, *Meditations*, 103–4.

51. For men, RRP 1:40; for women, RRP 2:43.

52. For men, RRP 1:53; for women, RRP 2:58.

53. For men, RRP 1:54; the significantly different text for women is "We ask for perseverance in following Christ our bridegroom in this religious community all the days of our lives," RRP 2:59.

54. For men, RRP 1:60; the significantly different text for women is ". . . let us pray to God the Father who gives us everything that is good; in his mercy may he strengthen his servants in the purpose he has inspired in them," RRP 2:65.

55. For men, RRP 1:59; for women, RRP 2:64.

56. RFR, n. 139.

57. RRL, n. 2.

58. Rahner, "On the Evangelical Counsels," 164.

59. Rahner, *Meditations*, vii.

60. Rahner, *Meditations*, 94.

61. Finkenzeller, *Die Lehre von den Sakramenten im allgemeinen von der Schrift bis zur Scholastik*, 72–72, 91–123 and 158–72.

62. See Emile de Backer, *Sacramentum, le mot et l'idée représentée par lui dans les oeuvres de Tertullien* (Louvain: Université de Louvain, 1911), especially 61–65; also, C. Mohrmann, "*Sacramentum* dans les plus anciens textes chrétiens," *Harvard Theological Review* 47 (1954), 141–52.

63. See, for example, Hugh of St. Victor, *De Sacramentis* 1.9.7 (PL 176:327).

64. Session 7, 3 March 1547, canon 3 (DENZ., n. 846).

65. Session 13, 11 October 1551 (DENZ., n. 876).

66. Session 6, chapter 7, 13 January 1547 (DENZ., n. 799).

67. *Christian Initiation*, General Introduction, n. 3. (DOL, n. 2252).

68. CSL, n. 2 (DOL, n. 2).

69. *Inter Oecumenici: Instruction on the orderly carrying out of the Constitution on the Liturgy*, n. 6 (DOL, n. 298).

70. Rahner, *The Church and the Sacraments*, 70–71.

71. Boff, *God's Witnesses in the Heart of the World*, 23.

72. These will be explored in chapter 3.

73. Karl Rahner, "How to Receive a Sacrament and Mean It," in *The Sacraments*, ed. Michael J. Taylor (Staten Island: Alba House, 1981), 73.

74. Epistola 61.2 (PL 33:229); for a discussion of the flexible meaning of sacrament in Augustine, and a relatively exhaustive listing of references, see C. Coutourier, "'Sacramentum' et 'Mysterium' dans l'oeuvre de Saint Augustine," in *Etudes Augustiniennes* (Paris: Aubier, 1953), 161–301.

75. *De Ecclesiastica Hierarchia* 6:3 (PG 3:533).

76. *Epistola* 165 (PG 99:1524).

77. *Opuscula* 13.6 (PL 145:300); *Opuscula* 16.8 (PL 145:376–77); also, see Pseudo-Peter Damian, *Sermo* 69 (PL 144:901).

78. *De Sacramentis* 1.9.7 (PL 176:327).

79. Ghellinck, *Le Mouvement théologique*, 539.

80. Martin Jugie, *Theologia Dogmatica Christianorum Orientalium*, Vol. 3: *Theologiae dogmaticae Graeco-Russorum expositio de Sacramentis* (Paris: Letouzey, 1930), 17.

81. *De Sacramentis* 52 (PG 155:198).

82. See, for example, Casel, "Die Mönchsweihe bei St. Benedikt," passim.

83. Schillebeeckx, *Christ the Sacrament*, 66.

84. I am grateful to my colleague, Kathleen Hughes, RSCJ, for raising this question for me.

85. Compare, for example, the solemn blessings for men (RRP 1:67) and for women (RRP 2:72).

The Pastoral Implications

Having outlined the reasons why religious profession can and should be understood in a sacramental framework, we now address the pastoral consequences of this understanding. These consequences are intimately related to the sacramental definition that we predicated of religious profession and flow from the very nature of sacrament.

A contemporary understanding of sacrament begins with Christ who is the primordial sacrament and extends to the church, the sacrament of Christ. Individuals are drawn into a relationship with God through Christ, who is present to the world in a special way through the life of the church and particularly through the church's worship. In Rahner's language, sacrament presumes the offer of redemptive grace (in Christ),[1] which at once respects the true nature of the church and simultaneously engages the individual in an unconditional offer of salvation.[2] Thus, a holistic approach to sacrament has a christological dimension, an ecclesial dimension and a particular or individual dimension.

Religious profession is similarly an act of Christ, an act of the church and a particular act of an individual within a specific faith community. Each of these dimensions, however, implies certain formational and ritual consequences. As we explore these, we will pay particular attention to parallels between religious profession and ecclesial initiation—especially as embodied in the RCIA—which historically, theologically and ritually has been so determinative in the development of religious life and its rituals.

Profession as an Act of Christ

It was Pius XII who clearly articulated for the 20th century church the principle that all worship is first of all an act of Christ. In his 1947 encyclical *Mediator Dei* he wrote:

> The sacred liturgy is . . . the public worship which our Redeemer as head of the church renders to the Father as well as the worship which the community of the faithful renders to its founder, and through him to the heavenly Father.[3]

This principle, reiterated many times and in many forms since Pius XII, is foundational for the liturgical theology expressed in the Constitution on the Sacred Liturgy, which notes that "public worship is performed by the mystical body of Jesus Christ, that is, by the Head and his members," and again that every liturgical celebration is "an action of Christ the priest and of his body which is the church."[4] This is another way of acknowledging that every sacrament begins in Jesus Christ, who is properly understood as the first of all sacraments.

Specifically this means that the eucharist, for example, is not merely a celebration of *our* communion with each other or primarily *our* offering of praise and thanksgiving, but, as articulated by the Council of Trent and reiterated in the General Instruction of the Roman Missal, it is "first and foremost, the action of Christ himself."[5] Baptism, as well, is not principally our definitive declaration of faith, but is that act whereby we are joined to Christ's dying and rising[6] and celebrate the memorial of his death and resurrection.[7] Christian marriage, too, is not only a human event whose content is the public proclamation of love, but is a divine-human event that signifies and shares in "the mystery of the unity and fruitful love that exists between Christ and his church."[8] Consequently, sacraments in their origin and essence are Christ events. This is summarized in the *General Catechetical Directory:*

> Sacraments are the principal and fundamental actions whereby Jesus Christ unceasingly bestows his Spirit on the faithful, thus making them the holy people which offers itself, in him and with him, as an oblation acceptable to the Father. To the church, then, belongs the power of administering them; and yet they are always to be referred to Christ, from whom they receive their efficacy.[9]

The act of religious profession, as well, must be recognized as an action of Christ. At its root it is neither a celebration of personal achievement nor a pseudograduation ceremony from the rigors of initial formation. Rather, religious profession—as a sacramental and therefore christological event—finds its first meaning in the action of Christ, and only then in the act of those to be professed. The introduction to the Rite of Religious Profession notes that profession (like marriage), is nothing other than "a sign of the unbreakable union between Christ and his bride the church."[10] As further elaborated in the preface for Masses of Religious Profession, this ritual act is first and foremost one of giving thanks and praise "through Jesus Christ . . . [who] taught by his whole life the perfection of chastity, [who] became obedient even to dying for us . . . [and who] consecrated more closely to [God's] service those who leave all things for your sake."[11]

This christological focus has profound formational and ritual consequences. Because the purpose of initial religious formation is to prepare one to "follow Christ more closely through the evangelical counsels,"[12] formation itself has a christological focus. This does not mean that religious formation needs to be explicitly concerned with the theological discipline of christology, but instead with the cultivation of a personal and lifelong relationship with Jesus Christ. Consequently, just as the basic journey of the catechumen is movement toward that "true and living faith by which they hold fast to Christ,"[13] so is every form of religious life " ordered to the following of Christ."[14]

In making this assertion we do not deny that each community has its own proper character and mission, particular goals and founding spirit that constitute its unique heritage.[15] Each particular heritage, however, must be harmonized with that central call to imitation of Christ, for "the final norm of the religious life is the following of Christ as put before us in the gospel: This must be taken by all institutes as the supreme law."[16] Only such a perspective respects the tradition that acknowledges the following of Christ as not only at the very origin of religious life[17] but the basis for the call to holiness extended to the whole church.[18]

This christological bias in religious formation has clear ritual consequences, both for the entirety of the initial formation journey as well as for the profession ritual itself. Fundamental here is the presumption that religious formation must give a certain priority to the official liturgy of the church that itself embodies our basic spirituality. Such a presumption acknowledges that the church's liturgy, which the Second Vatican Council has called the "summit toward which the activity of the church is directed . . . [and] the fount from which all her power flows,"[19] is a privileged means for encountering and adhering to the Christ who is the center of all religious life. It seems appropriate to consider the church's liturgy not only as our first theology,[20] but also as our first "catechesis": leading the believer into the heart of the paschal mystery where Christ is authentically encountered and where we are invited and formed to be like him in all things.

Because the public worship of the church is foundational for our common faith and commitment and therefore of our common spirituality, it sets the standard for all our prayer. The Constitution on the Sacred Liturgy notes that every kind of prayer and devotion should "harmonize with the liturgical seasons, accord with the sacred liturgy, be in some way derived from it, and lead the people to it, since the liturgy by its very nature far surpasses any of them."[21] Beyond assenting to the centrality of the church's official worship in the journey toward final profession, the formation process must embody this ideal by securely grounding the candidate in the church's liturgy. This is clearly the intent of the Second Vatican Council, which called religious to "assiduously cultivate the spirit of prayer and prayer itself, drawing on the authentic sources of Christian spirituality," which the Council further defines as sacred scripture and the sacred liturgy.[22]

Therefore the Liturgy of the Hours, as the daily prayer of the whole people of God, should hold an important place in a candidate's developing prayer life. As the Apostolic Constitution of Paul VI, *Laudis Canticum*, remarks, "It is to be hoped above all that the liturgy of the hours may pervade and penetrate the whole of Christian prayer, giving it life, direction and expression and effectively nourishing the spiritual life of the people of God."[23]

The eucharist is at the very core of the church's life[24] and by consequence central to every formation process within the church. "All other liturgical rites and all the works of the Christian life are linked with the eucharistic celebration, flow from it, and have it as their end."[25] Eucharist is at the heart of ecclesial and religious initiation. Both the celebration and spirituality of the eucharist are rich matter for the formation of religious candidates.

Though it would be possible to highlight many aspects of the church's worship that could contribute to the formation of fully initiated religious, it seems important to underscore the significance of the liturgical year in developing an authentic liturgical spirituality. As well demonstrated by the RCIA, it is through the various seasons of the year that "the church unfolds the entire mystery of Christ . . . [and] in accord with traditional discipline, carries out the formation of the faithful."[26] This yearly journey "opens to the faithful the riches of the Lord's power and merits so that these are in some way made present in every age in order that the faithful may lay hold on them and be filled with saving grace."[27] A formation process oblivious to the rhythms of the liturgical year is deprived of that cyclic renewal in death and resurrection that nourishes the whole church.

There are specific consequences of the christological focus for the profession ritual itself. We instinctively know the difference between baptisms that focus on cute infants and those that, in the context of an adult faith, celebrate new life through the death and resurrection of Jesus Christ. We similarly understand the difference between weddings that are more a fashion show than the proclamation of marriage as a sacramental mirror of the love that Christ has for the church. So must we be able to distinguish between profession ceremonies that focus on those to be professed and those that are directed to the one who is the object of every faithful profession. This is the difference between professions that appear as minor coronations and those that are humble acts of thanksgiving for the initiative of God's graciousness in Christ—the difference between profession as congratulatory and profession as a creedal proclamation of one's absolute willingness to follow Christ.

Various elements in the profession ritual can support or undermine this christological perspective. These include the wide-ranging possibilities in readings, prayers and music that shape and accompany such rites. For example, readings such as the christological hymns in Philippians 2:6–11 ("He emptied himself and took the form of a slave") or Colossians 1:15–20 ("He is the image of the invisible God") can serve to underscore that religious profession—like religious life itself—is a Christ event. On the other hand, a text such as Isaiah 61:1–9 ("The spirit of the Lord is upon me") or Revelation 19:1, 5–9 ("Happy are they invited to the wedding feast of the lamb") might appear to emphasize the importance of the candidate for profession and underemphasize the christological nature of this event.

One might similarly distinguish between psalmody that could be construed as announcing individual achievement (e.g., Psalm 1, "Happy is the one who follows not the counsel of the wicked") and that which more obviously celebrates the wonder of our God (e.g., Psalm 84, "How lovely is your dwelling place"). Musically, as well, one understands the difference between "Here I am, Lord" and "Cry out with joy to the Lord all the earth," between "This is the feast of victory" and "Now thank we all our God." Such is not to suggest that (aside from the important questions of musical quality) these are not valuable scriptural or lyrical texts. Rather, the ritual texts play an important role in shaping the personality of a rite and need to be considered seriously when such rites are in preparation. One community's guide to the rites of profession comments:

> Although we would not plan a ceremony of profession which would deliberately and obviously present a false view of religious life, it is possible that the rite convey such a view either implicitly or in subtle ways. Consequently, we must be conscious of the implications of our signs and prayers so that they may be the expression of a rich understanding of religious life.[28]

The power of preaching in shaping the tone and focus of a profession ritual should not be underestimated. The intent and content of the homily should be given serious consideration. A baptismal homily is not primarily congratulatory to the neophyte but a proclamation of the paschal mystery reborn in this initiate. A funeral homily is not a eulogy but an announcement of death vanquished and Christ risen. So profession preaching is not a commencement address or canonization sermon but a witness to the mystery of God's fidelity in Christ, embodied in candidate and community.

The ritual's preference for the celebration of final profession within the context of the eucharist[29] is especially noteworthy when attempting to achieve an appropriate christological center in these rites. As eucharist is the central sacramental act of the church, and in its essence is an act of Christ, so does eucharist present itself as the paradigmatic context for religious profession. The necessary role of the hierarchical priesthood—which might at first seem at odds with the act of religious profession—does not render the eucharist an inappropriate setting for this ritual act. Though attention should be paid to the essentially nonhierarchical nature of profession[30] and the clerical ministries need to be nuanced in light of this ritual,[31] eucharist itself—as the action of Christ and source of the church's life—is to be presumed as the normative ritual context for religious profession.

Profession as an Act of the Church

It has been the church's constant, if sometimes overlooked, teaching that all sacraments—besides being acts of Christ—are also acts of the church. This belief was intrinsic to an emerging sacramental system that understood worship as a corporate act of the whole body of Christ. It was embedded in our law that required the intention of the church even in the most private sacramental actions. It has found a more explicit voice in Pius XII's previously cited definition of liturgy. Therein he defines liturgy not only as the worship that Christ renders to the one he called Father but also the worship "which the community of the faithful renders to its founder, and through him to the heavenly Father."[32] All liturgy, of which sacraments are a specific type, is undeniably ecclesial.

Various ritual reforms in the past two decades have attempted to respect this ecclesial dimension of our sacramental life with varying degrees of success. Notable here is the third option in the Rite of Penance, reconciliation of penitents with general confession and absolution. Though severely restricted in practice, this rite uniquely demonstrates what the introduction to the Rite of Penance identifies as the special role of the "whole church" in reconciliation: calling sinners to repentance, interceding for them, helping them to acknowledge sin and becoming themselves the very instrument of conversion and absolution.[33]

More than any other of the reformed rites, the RCIA clearly testifies to the ecclesial nature of a sacrament. Private instruction in the rectory gives way to a process of transformation "within the community of the faithful."[34] An individual act of cleansing is now a central event for all of the faithful.[35] What was once an essentially clerical act has become the assembly's reaffirmation of belief on the holiest night of the year. The RCIA has illustrated with unparalleled clarity that initiation into the death and resurrection of Christ is achieved through the sacramentality of the church.

The act of religious profession is also a profoundly ecclesial act. This dimension of profession has a firm theological foundation in the teaching that it is none other than the church itself that receives the vows of those who make profession.[36] This is a ritual extension of the conviction that religious life belongs inseparably to the church's life and holiness and that perpetual profession is a sign of the "unbreakable bond of union that exists between Christ and his bride the church."[37]

The ecclesial nature of religious profession implies significant formational and ritual consequences. Formation not only enables candidates to cultivate a personal and lifelong relationship with Christ and initiates them into the charism and mission of their own particular community but must also call them to be ecclesial people.[38] As articulated by the Second Vatican Council, religious—even those leading cloistered lives—cannot be separated from the church in or by their life in religion. Instead, "the evangelical counsels unite those who practice them to the church and her mystery in a special way. . . . [Therefore] such Christians should be dedicated . . . to the welfare of the entire church."[39]

Those charged with leadership in religious formation must always be cautious of fostering, even indirectly, a sense of elitism "as though it (i.e., religious life) were a kind of middle way between the clerical and lay conditions of life"[40] or a way to greater holiness apart from baptism. Instead, the words of the Dogmatic Constitution on the Church (DCC) should ring in the ears of every candidate for religious life: "It is . . . quite clear that all Christians in any state or walk of life are called to the fullness of Christian life and to the perfection of love."[41] Religious life is not better or worse than any other Christian way of life: It is just different.

Religious formation that acknowledges the underlying ecclesial nature of religious life therefore must prepare candidates for cooperation with and service to all the baptized.[42] Religious formation need not mimic the process of RCIA and can offer models that will strengthen the RCIA. Though the RCIA's instructions on the catechumenate, for example, presume that catechumens should "learn how to work actively with others to spread the gospel and build up the church by the testimony of their lives and by profession of their faith,"[43] in practice this vital formational task is often ignored. Consequently, the RCIA process sometimes becomes focused on the personal conversion of the individual candidate without a broader view of mission and apostolic responsibility to the wider church. Here religious formation can inform catechumenal formation by demonstrating that inviting candidates into a personal encounter with Jesus Christ is simultaneously an invitation into the service enacted by his church.

Such an ecclesial perspective has an impact upon the liturgical life of those in initial formation. Liturgical formation must not breed a separatist spirit or sense of elitism among the candidates but prepare them for cooperation with and service to the wider ecclesial community. Particular devotions or prayer styles that are related to the spirit or charisms of individual religious communities should not degenerate into a form of liturgical elitism that bars entry to the faithful.

Concretely, the vernacular of the church's public worship must become an integral part and mainstay of every religious community's common prayer. The liturgy of the hours, which is considered "the prayer of the church with Christ and to Christ,"[44] belongs in the active repertory of every religious. Only then can religious fulfill their mandate to "see to it that people are invited and prepared . . . to celebrate the principal hours in common."[45] Thus are religious communities "advised to celebrate some parts of the liturgy of the hours, in accordance with their own situation, for it is the prayer of the church and makes the whole church, scattered throughout the world, one in heart and mind."[46]

Integrating the liturgy of the hours into the vocabulary of a religious community presumes more than an ability to find one's place in an official book and read the prescribed text. It means comprehension of the structure and content of the hours. It means recognizing the difference between what are sometimes called "monastic" and "cathedral" styles of celebrating the hours,[47] understanding the difference between primary and secondary elements in the hours[48] and developing abilities in liturgical preparation and leadership so that this is not an inaccessible prayer of the specialists but the praise of the whole church. All of this requires competent and thorough instruction during the period of initial formation.

The ecclesial nature of the profession rite is well reflected in the rite itself.[49] Its eucharistic context, the call and examination of the candidate and the continuous petition on the part of the community manifest that religious profession is an official invitation and acceptance of the mission of the church. This mission is to "build up the church, advance the salvation of the world, and be a convincing sign of the blessings of the world to come."[50] This ecclesial commission and commitment is confirmed by the church, which receives the vows of those who make profession.[51]

Because the church is a primary actor in rites of religious profession, these rites cannot be privatized or held captive by the personal whim of those who plan them. There is, for example, a presumed and focal role for the major superior, who personifies in a special way this broader ecclesial dimension.

Major superiors are not only central to the profession ceremony but are also intimately engaged in the preparation of such rites.

The ecclesial nature of these rites also requires that they be accessible not only to the religious community but also to the broader community of the faithful. These rites should be scheduled so that appropriate members of the family and local church, as well as collaborators in ministry, can be present.[52] The content and shape of the rites must render them accessible to the baptized as well as to the religious community. Religious profession is not a mystery rite, filled with obscure imagery and impenetrable customs that reduce the assembly to speechless wonder. Rather, like every other liturgical event of the contemporary church, the rites "should be marked by a noble simplicity; they should be short, clear and unencumbered by useless repetition; they should be within the people's powers of comprehension and as a rule not require much explanation."[53]

The whole assembly must be able to participate in the rites. The faithful cannot be reduced to informed but silent spectators who watch the religious community perform: The active participation of the whole gathered community is a hallmark and presumption of the reform.[54] As with ecclesial initiation, the faith of the whole church—and not that of some privileged group within the church—is foundational for this worship. That faith should be given voice and affirmation. Rites of profession should be marked by an inclusivity in language, ritual and ministry that demonstrates how religious profession is an authentically ecclesial act.[55]

Profession as a Particular Act

Religious profession is intrinsically christological and ecclesial, but it also has a particular and personal nature. Sacraments are first of all acts of Christ in and through the church, but every sacrament exists only through a particular community and specific individuals. Every sacrament is a source of grace for both individual and community.[56] Though of divine initiative, they need to be completed by a human action.[57] As summarized in an ancient liturgical proverb, "Sacraments are for people."[58]

Over the centuries the church has attempted in various ways to maintain a balanced understanding of sacraments as both ecclesial and individual actions. These complementary components are reflected in the dialogical structure of virtually every Christian liturgy. Our worship is an interplay of God's invitation and our response, of presidential prayer and the community's assent, of the proclamation of salvation in Christ and the personal "Amen."

Theologically, this dynamic has traditionally been expressed in the complementary (though sometimes misunderstood) axioms *ex opere operato* and *ex opere operantis*: The former attests to the fidelity of God in every sacramental enterprise through the mediation of the community, and the latter confirms our freedom to respond or reject this call. When isolated from each other, these proverbs (especially the former) have sometimes been interpreted in a magical sense, giving rise to the belief that grace is conferred merely by the proper execution of the ritual, regardless of the disposition or intention of the sacramental candidate. Authentic sacrament requires more: the dialogue of call and response, God's fidelity and our free assent. Only then can sacrament be considered a sign of "Christ's redemptive act in its actual grasp of a particular individual."[59] For example, every baptism objectively signifies initiation through the church into the death and resurrection of Christ, but it must always be achieved through the mediation of a particular community with the faithful assent of the elect.

Religious profession is also such an act. In response to the initiative of God in Christ and the mediation of the church, profession is always and only a particular woman or man who professes a life of poverty, chastity and obedience in the context of a given community. It is only when such an individual makes this response that sacrament occurs in the most complete sense. Every form of religious life ". . . is ordered to the following of Christ."[60] Thus religious profession is the declaration of a particular believer who is willing and eager to follow Christ through the vowed life, a declaration that is accepted and affirmed by the church.

The formational consequences of this realization are manifold. If religious formation takes the individuality of each candidate seriously, then formation cannot be achieved merely by marching candidates through an unvarying program on a predetermined timetable. Religious formation is not a program but a process.[61]

The RCIA is enormously instructive in both its attentiveness to the nature of this journey and in its flexibility in time and content to such a process. The very structure of the RCIA affirms that initiation is not a series of rituals to be endured, nor a course in catechism to be passed, but a process of conversion punctuated by rites. This process clearly progresses from precatechumenate to catechumenate to election to initiation to mystagogy, with specific goals predicated at each stage in the process. Becoming a catechumen presumes that an individual manifests the beginnings of a prayer life and spiritual life, understands the fundamentals of Christian teaching, has experienced an initial conversion and the first stirring of repentance and has had some experience of the Christian community.[62] The time it takes an individual to achieve this growth is not rigidly established. As the rite notes about the catechumenal period:

> The duration of the catechumenate will depend on the grace of God and on various circumstances, such as the program of instruction for the catechumenate, the number of catechists, deacons and priests, the cooperation of the individual catechumens, the means necessary for them to come to the site of the catechumenate and spend time there, the help of the local community. Nothing, therefore, can be settled *a priori*.[63]

There are various stages in the process of religious formation, each with its own goals and expectations. Furthermore, there are certainly some parallels between the various stages that prepare one for ecclesial initiation and those that prepare one for full initiation into a religious community.[64] Initiation into religious life, however, presumes the basic faith development embodied in ecclesial initiation, so the rites and processes of the RCIA cannot be borrowed in their entirety for religious formation. Principles of process and individuation need to be respected.

In the final preparation of those elected for Easter initiation, the church celebrates scrutinies on the Third, Fourth and Fifth Sundays of Lent. These public rituals include an exorcism and a blessing. The church prays that the elect might be purified from what is evil and confirmed in virtue. These rituals presumably mirror the conversion process itself in which the candidates struggle against sin and grow in grace. Candidates for initiation into religious life also undergo a series of evaluations or public scrutinies in their journey toward vows. They might benefit from the basic dynamics embodied in the catechumenal scrutinies, but the evaluations or scrutinies of religious are different from those found in the RCIA. They usually are not restricted to the time before final incorporation but occur on a yearly basis beginning with preparation for novitiate, then first profession and renewal of vows, and at last perpetual profession. Though such scrutinies are often an integral component of the formational process, they seldom are conducted in the context of liturgical prayer. Inspired and informed by the RCIA, however, religious communities could develop scrutinies that would punctuate the yearly rites of passage (especially the somewhat anomalous process of the renewal of vows). Through rites of exorcism and blessing, the community would pray that candidates might be purified from evil and confirmed in virtue. Such a ritual process might include the renewal of vows as a special confirmation of virtue, foreshadowing final confirmation in perpetual profession.[65]

Whatever the adaptation, each religious community should clarify the various stages in the formational journey toward full initiation and shape this process so that it respects both the charism of the community and the individuality of each candidate. Each community needs to discover how it can effectively ritualize the movement through this process from one stage to another.[66] Such adaptation should respect both the nature of religious initiation and each individual's initiation as a particular act.

Religious profession as the particular act of an individual within a specific community has clear consequences for the profession ritual. There is the recognition that sacramental candidates are never merely "acted upon" by the church. They are to be fully engaged in the ritual event. Like those to be initiated or married, candidates for religious profession have a role to play in the rites. The need for such involvement is underscored by Eric Meyer's contention: "The candidate for the religious life is the minister of this sacrament."[67] Mere visibility or audibility is inadequate. The profession liturgy must take the individual seriously. Opportunities within the rites should allow the individuals to express their faith and commitment. The call and examination of the candidates, for example, can be adapted to the needs and personality of each candidate. The models provided in the official ritual need not simply be parroted. Their form suggests that the community, through its leaders, have a prepared dialogue with the candidate which reflects the willingness and ability of both to enter into this final act of incorporation.

In the judicious shaping of ministries, profession candidates can find an active and appropriate role in the worship. Who better, for example, to be ministers of hospitality this day than those being fully initiated into a life of service? Or who better to minister communion than those who identify themselves anew with the body of Christ? Those to be professed should not dominate the ministries, but as adult Christians, they should be perceived as central actors in this sacramental action: an action that must mirror their individual spirit as well as the spirit of the sponsoring community. A profession ritual that does not reflect such individuality is inattentive to those who make profession and to that extent could be considered unauthentic ritual.

Summary

Like every true symbol, public worship both expresses and creates. In the words of the Constitution on the Sacred Liturgy, liturgy is both font and summit of our faith and our life as church. This chapter has attempted to take seriously this expressive and creative function of worship as it relates to religious profession. The demand for integrity in our worship reaches far beyond the ritual moment into the remote preparation before and the consequent living after such ritual. To disconnect ritual from this "before and after" is either to rob it of its power or allow it to degenerate into magic.

Religious profession, as a christological, ecclesial and particular act, demands integrity. We have sketched here some specific formational and ritual examples that reach toward such integrity. This is intended only to be illustrative. The goal has not been new rules for religious formation and ritual expression but understanding how our worship is itself the first rule of faith. Religious formation and ritual expression that respect and acknowledge this will have discovered an authentic way for understanding and living religious life.

Notes

1. Rahner clearly links redemptive grace with Christ, noting, for example, that the "absolute and irrevocable self-communication of God to the spiritual creature . . . is finally established through its goal and climax, i.e., through incarnation." "Christology within an evolutionary view," *Theological Investigations*, Vol. 5: *Later Writings*, trans. Karl-H. Kruger (Baltimore: Helicon Press, 1966), 186.

2. See above, 43–48

3. *Mediator Dei*, n. 20 (Denz., n. 2298).

4. CSL, n. 7 (DOL, n. 7).

5. GIRM Introduction, n. 11 (DOL, n. 1386); also see n. 54 (DOL, n. 1443).

6. CSL, n. 6 (DOL, n. 6).

7. Christian Initiation, General Introduction, n. 1.

8. Rite of Marriage, n. 1 (DOL, n. 2969).

9. GCD, n. 55 (DOL, n. 1102).

10. RRP, n. 6; this text is reliant upon DCC, n. 44.

11. RRP Appendix, 213.

12. RRP, n. 1, 115.

13. *Christian Initiation*, General Introduction, n. 3.

14. RRL, n. 2e (VC II, 613).

15. RRL, n. 2b (VC II, 612).

16. RRL, n. 2a (VC II, 612).

17. RRL, n. 1 (VC II, 611).

18. DCC, n. 40 (VC II, 397).

19. CSL, n. 10 (DOL, n. 10).

20. See above, 41.

21. CSL, n. 13 (DOL, n. 13).

22. RRL, n. 6 (VC II, 614).

23. *Laudis Canticum*, n. 8 (DOL, n. 3426).

24. CSL, n. 10 (DOL, n. 10).

25. GIRM, 1.1 (DOL, n. 1391).

26. General Norms for the Liturgical Year and the Calendar, n. 1 (DOL, n. 3767).

27. CSL, n. 102 (DOL, n. 102).

28. The Committee for Franciscan Liturgical Research, *Entering the Order of Friars Minor: Background Information and Liturgical Guidelines* (Pulaski, Wisconsin: Franciscan Publishers, 1979), 18.

29. RRP, n. 6.

30. DCC, n. 44; also, RRL, n. 43.

31. Consequently, concelebration is often an inappropriate gesture at such a eucharist. On this topic, see John Baldovin, "Concelebration: A Problem of Symbolic Roles in the Church," *Worship* 59 (1985), 32–47.

32. *Mediator Dei*, n. 20 (DENZ., n. 2298).

33. Rite of Penance, Introduction, n. 8 (DOL, n. 3073).

34. RCIA Introduction, n. 4.

35. RCIA Introduction, n. 4.

36. RRP Introduction, n. 2.

37. DCC, n. 44 (VC II, 404).

38. RRL, n. 2 (VC II, 612).

39. DCC, n. 44 (VC II, 404).

40. DCC, n. 44 (VC II, 403).

41. DCC, n. 40 (VC II, 397).

42. RRL, n. 2 (VC II, 638).

43. RCIA, n. 75.4.

44. GILH, n. 2 (DOL, n. 3432).

45. GILH, n. 23 (DOL, n. 3453).

46. GILH, n. 32 (DOL, n. 3462).

47. See, for example, William Storey, "The Liturgy of the Hours: Cathedral versus Monastery," *Christians at Prayer*, ed. John Gallen (Notre Dame: University of Notre Dame Press, 1977), 61–82.

48. See, for example, Andrew Ciferni, "The Structure and Content of the Church's Daily Celebration of Time," *Worship* 54 (1980), 331–35.

49. See above, 43-44.

50. RRP 1:67.

51. RRP Introduction, n. 2.

52. RRP Introduction, n. 6.

53. CSL, n. 34 (DOL, n. 34).

54. CSL, n. 14 (DOL, n. 14); also see Frederick R. McManus, *Liturgical Participation: An Assessment*, American Essays in Liturgy 9 (Washington, D.C.: Pastoral Press, 1988).

55. Examples of such adaptation are given in chapter 5.

56. GCD, n. 56 (DOL, n. 1103).

57. Paul VI, "Address to a meeting of the presbyterate of Rome, on pastoral effectiveness in the ritual use of the sacraments" (DOL, n. 2242).

58. This axiom is echoed in the Statement of the United States Bishops' Committee on the Liturgy's, *Environment and Art in Catholic Worship*, n. 4.

59. Schillebeeckx, *Christ the Sacrament*, 81.

60. RRL 2e (VC II, 613).

61. See, for example, RRL, especially nn. 4, 5, 6, 10 (VC II, 639–45).

62. RCIA, n. 42.

63. RCIA, n. 76.

64. See, for example, Charles E. Bouchard, "Initial Religious Formation as an Extension of the New Rite of Initiation for Adults," *Review for Religious* 36 (1977), 592–99; and Thomas Krosnicki, "Christian Initiation of Adults and the Formation of Religious," *Review for Religious* 41 (1982), 867–87.

65. For an example of such a ritual process, see chapter 5.

66. See, for example, the previously cited *Entering the Order of Friars Minor: Background Information and Liturgical Guidelines.*

67. Meyer, "Is Religious Life a Sacrament?" 1115.

Preparing the Rites

The church believes that liturgy has the power to shape and express faith. The source of this power is certainly the abiding spirit of Jesus and the community's intention of faithfulness to his spirit. Liturgy also needs our ability to symbolize effectively this abiding spirit and the community's intention in worship. As the American bishops noted: "To celebrate the liturgy means to do the action or perform the sign in such a way that the full meaning and impact shine forth in clear and compelling fashion."[1] Careful preparation of all rites, including profession, is essential. Though such preparation will not ensure effective ritual, it is a most important step toward achieving this goal.

This chapter is an introduction to the preparation process for the rites of profession. Preparing the rites of profession is similar to preparing other liturgical rites, so our first task is to outline a basic process for liturgical preparation. Once this has been completed, we will offer a brief commentary on each rite of profession. In the next chapter we will outline specific ritual models for perpetual profession and the renewal of vows. The creation of individual models, however, is not so critical as the shaping of the entire rite that occupies us in this chapter.

The Preparation Process

There are a variety of approaches to the preparation of a single celebration or season. Many of the better processes address similar issues.[2] The outline given here will serve as a checklist of the basic issues that must be considered in the preparation of every ritual. It is a framework for discussing the preparation of the various profession liturgies.

Our process involves nine steps. These are discussed in their order of importance to the planning process. In every use of these steps, some issues will need to be discussed concurrently while some decisions must precede others and become formative for those that follow. Given the circumstances, the chronology of this process should be respected insofar as that is possible. Within each step, those responsible should first uncover and discuss various alternatives, then select the most appropriate. Without this effort there is the tendency to repeat last year's formula or to rely on liturgical cliches.

Context

In the beginning it is helpful to understand the broad context and specific setting of the worship. Study the rite, its structure and theology. Identify the primary and secondary elements in the liturgy.[3] Know how this rite relates to the rest of the church's worship and learn something of its history. Explore also the social and ecclesial setting for this rite. What is the place and time of the worship, and who will be in attendance? Has this assembly ever gathered before? Do they share a common culture? Are they acquainted with the rites? One needs to acquire a good sense of this liturgical and social context before the first hymn or scriptural text is chosen. Such will help to ensure the preparation of hospitable and authentic worship.

For the rites of profession, this means recognizing the distinctions between temporary and perpetual vows.[4] One must respect also the differences between contemplative and missionary communities, between clerical and nonclerical congregations. Will the rite take place within the context of eucharist or the liturgy of the hours? Is the setting a parish church or a convent chapel? Is the sponsoring religious community an American foundation or an international society?

Liturgy is not found in books. It is enacted by real people, in concrete situations, in light of our liturgical traditions. Respecting the social and ecclesial setting for each rite will prevent worship from collapsing into a string of quotations from approved books.

Texts

After considering the context of the ritual, study the many texts that punctuate each liturgy. Readings from scripture are focal and many people shape the preparation around them. Many other texts should be studied during this preparation. In the context of eucharist, prefaces and the various orations can reveal much about a given liturgy. Not to be overlooked are the variable texts proper to the specific rite being celebrated. These include vows at weddings, the commendation at funerals, and the thanksgiving for the light at vespers.

Multiple texts from the rites of profession deserve particular attention in the planning process. These include the various vow formulas and proper collects. For perpetual profession one should examine also the prayer of consecration and the litany of the saints. For temporary profession, scrutinize the examination and prayer for God's grace. Study of these texts will offer valuable insights into the nature of the celebration and raise questions about textual adaptation. Does the litany need to reflect more clearly the tradition of holiness within a specific congregation? Do the vow formulas need to be nuanced in view of a specific formation process or apostolic call? Attention to these kinds of questions transforms generic ritual into authentic celebration.

Central Rite(s)

After selecting and adapting the texts, consider the ritual shape of the liturgy. A common instinct in liturgical preparation is to plan a rite chronologically from opening rites to the dismissal. The problem with this linear approach is that it ignores the implied rhythm of each ritual and often produces elongated and undifferentiated ritual. It also creates what might be called a democratic planning style in which individual parts of equal value are considered in chronological succession. All ritual elements, however, are not of equal value. Planning should begin with the core elements.

To identify such rites, ask yourself: Are there some elements in this rite that, more than others, convey the essence of this worship? Is there a single ritual moment that most effectively interprets a specific ceremony? How can the liturgy allow this to happen? The rest of the worship can then be shaped to respect and complement this rite.

The profession of vows is a central rite. It should be discussed early in the planning process. Highlighting the vows can be achieved by three things: elaborating essential elements, downplaying secondary rites and eliminating accretions to the rite. The litany of all saints, for example, is the most important intercessory prayer before the profession. It requires appropriate elaboration with the prostration of the candidates, strong music and burning incense. Signing the document of profession, however, is an unnecessary accretion to the liturgy. Because enacting this canonical requirement in the midst of the rite detracts from the profession and undercuts the auditory nature of this event, it should be removed from the liturgy and done after the ceremony.

Shaping the vows in text and gesture must lead to connections with the rest of the rite. What are the verbal and nonverbal elements in the profession of vows that should echo through the rest of this liturgy? Are there ways that the gathering rites can mirror and evoke the profession of vows?[5] When this occurs, the ritual will achieve a marked degree of integrity and harmony.

Ministries

The United States Bishops' Committee on the Liturgy has observed: "No other single factor affects the liturgy as much as the attitude, style, and bearing of the celebrant."[6] To a lesser extent, this applies to all liturgical ministers. So that they do not overshadow the rite, it is wise to form the ministers in the image of the worship and not vice versa.

The church presumes that all ministers will do all and only those parts that belong to them.[7] This principle not only respects the variety of gifts within the community but also protects against the usurpation of the assembly's role. The liturgical assembly is primary in worship.[8] In some liturgical celebrations there are also sacramental candidates (to be initiated, married, ordained) who enjoy a special role within the assembly. These candidates are to appear as responsive adults in faith and not merely as objects of the church's attention and prayer. Candidates for the various rites of profession should be audible and visible in the worship without displacing other ministries.

In rites of profession, a certain ministerial balance is needed between the sponsoring religious community and the assembly, which may include some who are ordained. Achieving this balance can be especially difficult when profession in a lay institute occurs during the eucharist. In such circumstances the cooperative relationship of religious and clergy in the church's work must be reflected in the worship. The religious superior and eucharistic presider are collaborators in both and must make every effort to embody such mutuality in their respective ministries. If the eucharist is the context for religious profession,[9] the nature of this act as well as the distinct character of the consecrated life is well expressed without concelebration.

Homily

Only after the basic context, texts and ministries have been considered should one discuss the homily. The homily can draw together the various elements of the rite and articulate the significance of their conjunction. The homily should not be planned apart from these elements. As noted by the American bishops, "The very meaning and function of the homily is determined by its relation to the liturgical action of which it is a part."[10]

The homily is fundamentally not an explanation of the texts or gestures that form the rite. Rather, the homily is an interpretive act, inviting the assembly to a more complete faith response. Though it is important to have the sweep of the ritual in view when planning this event, it is not essential that every detail be resolved. Involving the homilist in a discussion of the homily in the early stages of preparation can effectively contribute to the evolving worship plan.

In the profession liturgy, it is crucial that the homilist attend to the christological, ecclesial and individual facets of the rite. The two extremes of canonizing or ignoring the candidates should be avoided. The homilist also needs to differentiate between the various stages of religious profession and guard against every impression that our response to God's invitation is ever complete. Finally, the homilist needs to keep in view the individual candidate, the religious community and the faithful who are present. The homilist must speak simply enough so those outside the religious community can enter with understanding. Simultaneously, the homilist needs to respect the specific charism of the religious community, for whom profession is a significant event. A member of the sponsoring religious community who knows the candidates and has a healthy ecclesiology may be the most appropriate homilist.

Contour of the Rites

Once the central rites have been shaped and the general direction of ministries and homily agreed upon, the contour of the whole rite needs to be established. This entails fashioning the secondary elements in such a way that they will complement and not overshadow the focal rites of the worship. Emphasizing the eucharistic prayer, for example, means not only attending to this prayer but also to the rites that precede and follow it. The preparation of the gifts cannot overshadow the eucharistic prayer in length or level of festivity. If it does, then despite any intention to the contrary, the preparation of the gifts will appear primary.

The profession of vows should not be overshadowed. They should also not render the rest of the worship anticlimactic. In the context of the eucharist this can be accomplished by doing three things. First, hold the introductory rites in check so they do not overshadow the liturgy of the word. Second, balance the liturgy of the word with the profession of vows and its accompanying rites so they appear as complementary elements. Third, elaborate the eucharistic prayer so it can be the "summit of the entire celebration."[11]

Music

Once the basic contour of the rite is in place, it is possible to select the music. This is not to suggest that music has been absent from all previous deliberations, for often the process of shaping the rites presupposes musical considerations. In general, however, it is good to delay a comprehensive discussion of the music until the ritual is in place.

Select first the music that will accompany the primary liturgical elements. Plan from the center out and shape secondary elements accordingly. Throughout this process one must decide both what will be sung and how it will be sung.

Early in the planning of rites of profession, consider the music for the profession of vows and the accompanying rites. Music is often absent from these rites: Typically, they then devolve into excessively verbal moments. The rite can be done with simple music to accompany the litany, the prayer of consecration and the presentation of the profession insignia. This music can also provide continuity between these various elements that together comprise a single ritual unit. One could, for example, employ variations on a single mantra or refrain during the litany, profession, prayer of consecration and presentation of insignia.[12]

Environment

Questions about the environment for worship, like those about the music, permeate the entire preparation process. These are resolved toward the end of the process. This involves far more than passing attention to "decorations" and is first concerned with the very configuration of the worship space. Most worship spaces are designed for eucharistic liturgy and seldom attend to the spatial demands of other rituals. The primary task in preparing the environment, therefore, is fashioning the space so it respects and supports a specific kind of worship. Arrange the space so that ministers, sacramental candidates and assembly are audible and visible to each other throughout the rite.[13] This should be accomplished within a unified space that does not segregate one group from another.[14] Once the basic arrangement has been designed, consider the artifacts that will adorn the space. Here the principles articulated in Environment and Art in Catholic Worship need to be respected.[15]

Candidates for profession must be visible and audible during the central rites. The space also should allow the ministers, religious community and faithful to interact without exclusions. Never relegate the faithful to pews behind the religious community, visiting clergy or concelebrants. Their place should manifest their primary role in the worship.

As for the other appointments, the Rite of Religious Profession is a useful guide in its instruction on perpetual profession. There it notes that the service should be celebrated with fitting solemnity, avoiding any appearance of lavishness unbecoming to religious poverty.[16] This can be achieved by respecting the dual principles of quality and appropriateness articulated in Environment and Art in Catholic Worship.[17]

Continuity

Finally, one should review the entire plan for continuity so that the central texts, melodies and gestures are reiterated throughout the rite. At its root all ritual is repetitive. Liturgy, a genre of ritual, also needs to be repetitive. It is this repetition that creates the sense of trust and familiarity[18] that is essential for true participation. Monotony results only from poorly conceived repetition. Various art forms demonstrate that repetition with variation can achieve a satisfactory balance between the fresh and the familiar. Our worship must do the same.

This means rehearsing key texts from introductory rites to the final blessing. Musically it suggests reviewing the program for similarity in style and melody. This will prevent the worship from appearing as a string of unrelated musical fragments. Visually it presumes a certain complementarity between the vesture, decorations, specially prepared worship aids and invitations. To raise the question of continuity is simply to inquire whether the ritual is an integrated rite or only a series of assembled components.

Like weddings and other once-in-a-lifetime events, profession rites draw a congregation that never before and never again will assemble for worship. With such a group it is wise to provide an even higher level of continuity within the worship than in other situations. General unfamiliarity with the rites of profession could suggest a careful reiteration of key textual images or ritual ingredients throughout the worship. This might happily stifle the deadening practice of explaining the ritual symbols. The lack of a common musical vocabulary within the assembly might suggest an exceptional degree of continuity within the sung elements of the worship. Relying on self-rehearsing music could eliminate the need for any pre-liturgy practice. Everything should be done to make the ritual familiar and accessible to this one-time assembly.

The Rites of Profession

For each rite, elements of the previously outlined process that deserve special attention will be discussed.

The Rite of Initiation into the Religious Life

CONTEXT   Though this is not a rite of profession, it is an important stage in the journey toward perpetual profession. It should be planned in continuity with the other rites without prematurely anticipating them. The instruction notes: "The rite is to be very simple and direct in the presence of the religious community only."[19] The simplicity of this ritual is underscored by the proscription against celebrating this rite during the eucharist.[20] The rite, which takes place during a liturgy of the word, has the following structure:

Introductory Rites
[psalm/hymn]
[greeting]
question/response
prayer

Celebration of the Word
   scripture
   responsories
   address by superior
Conclusion of the Rite
   general intercessions
   Our Father
   closing prayer
   greeting of the candidates
   song

TEXTS   The rites of initiation for women and men are almost identical. The one notable exception is the text for the closing prayer.[21]

MEN	WOMEN
Lord God	God our Father
you call us to your service	it is you who have called us.
and inspire us to hear	Hear our prayers
your call.	and bless these sisters of ours
These brothers of ours	who wish to follow your son
desire to test our way of life:	in religious life.
help them to know what	Help us all to do what you
you ask of them	ask of us
and strengthen us all	so that your plans for them
in your service	may be fulfilled.
We ask this through Christ	We ask this through Christ
our Lord.	our Lord.
Amen.	Amen.

The male candidates are presented as active and responsible, the female candidates as passive respondents to the process. In shaping the texts for this rite, it is important to represent both male and female candidates as responsive adults.

CENTRAL RITE   Some elements in this rite, such as the scripture readings, are more important than others. The true focus of

83

this ritual, however, is not any single text or ritual gesture. Rather, it is the very gathering of the candidates in the embrace of the welcoming religious community. Overemphasizing any single element in this brief rite could distract from the centrality of this act. Ritual gestures should be simple, explanations should be eliminated and the music kept unpretentious. Nothing should undermine the simple embrace of this rite.

MINISTRY The introduction notes: "The texts for the rite must avoid anything that may seem to diminish the novices' freedom of choice or obscure the true meaning of a noviceship or time of testing."[22] Candidates can demonstrate their freedom by announcing their willingness to enter this way of life. The rite suggests that postulants say together a common formula of acceptance or have a representative speak for them.[23] It is stronger if each individual speaks separately. Because this ceremony marks the beginning of a testing period, however, it is best if the candidates assume a receptive stance during the majority of the rite. The restrained nature of the ceremony further suggests that the ministry should be kept to a minimum.

ADDRESS If the liturgy shapes the homily, then this liturgy calls for a simple word. Given the modesty of the rite, a lengthy word could become the prominent element. It is better to have a lean word that can extend the invitation without overshadowing the act of inviting.

MUSIC Music can be especially effective for providing a sense of richness to these bare rites. At the same time, one should guard against allowing the music to dominate. Eliminate all solo singing and concentrate on responsorial or hymnic forms. Both contribute to the communal nature of this liturgy. Because this rite announces the beginning of a period of testing, the texts of the music should avoid any inference of completion or accomplishment.

ENVIRONMENT   The introduction to this rite comments: "The chapter hall or other similar room is an appropriate setting for the rite. If it seems necessary, however, the rite may take place in the chapel."[24] Chapels or churches designed for the eucharist are not the preferred place for this rite. Their natural focus on altar, chair and ambo would not support the gathering nature of this ritual. A better environment is an open space where the community can figuratively and actually embrace the candidates. The community itself should be the primary environment in this ritual.

In summary, this rite gravitates toward understatement in texts, ministry and appointments. Such lean ritual does not necessarily translate into pragmatic or impersonal ceremony. Hospitality and simplicity should be the hallmarks.

The Rite of Temporary Profession

CONTEXT   Temporary profession is an unusual celebration of commitment without finality.[25] This paradox of first commitment without final commitment must be considered when preparing this rite. These contrasting elements send a mixed message about the personality of such celebrations. On the one hand, there is a public and festive side to this worship. This is a joyful rite to be celebrated by the regional religious community. Its public and festive nature far exceeds that of the Rite of Initiation into the Religious Life. On the other hand, this is not the full initiation that comes with perpetual profession. Consequently, it is a service of restrained joy.

This rite's structure reflects the basic outline that will mark every rite of profession. Within the context of the eucharist, this rite follows the gospel:

call/response
homily
examination
prayer

>   profession
>   presentation of insignia
>   conclusion

The rite for women also includes a blessing of the habit on the day before profession. This variation allows the candidates to wear the habit without the veil from the beginning of the profession service.[26] When the women receive the veil during the ritual, the men are clothed in the religious habit.[27]

TEXTS   The texts for the rite of temporary profession of men are significantly different from those for women. As previously noted, the texts for men's rites stress the apostolic nature of the commitment. Texts from the rites for women emphasize a passive-receptive nature of the commitment.[28] Compare the responses of men to women when asked "What do you ask of God and of his holy church?"

MEN
We ask for God's merciful
love and for the grace
   of serving him more
   perfectly in your
(this) religious community

WOMEN
We ask for God's merciful
love and a share in
   the life of this religious
   community of N.

Given this disparity, many have seen the need for revision of the texts.

CONTOUR OF THE RITES   The profession of vows is pivotal in these rites and should influence the shaping of the rest of the worship. The rite of temporary profession lacks many of the ancillary rites that accompany perpetual profession.[29] The scaled-down nature of these rites suggests a similar proportion for the rest of the celebration, which could be difficult in the context of the eucharist. Given the length of the eucharistic prayer and communion rites, it is easy to overshadow the act of profession. This could suggest a noneucharistic setting for temporary profession. Temporary profession within a non-eucharistic context like the liturgy of the hours could distinguish it from initiation (within a word service) and perpetual profession (within the eucharist).

MINISTRIES   The profession of temporary vows is an ecclesial act. The ministries for this service should reflect this ecclesial nature. The religious community has a central role here. There is also a special place in the ministry for the temporary professed in this service. To the extent that members of the wider church contributed to the initial formation process, so do they fulfill certain ministries here as well.

ENVIRONMENT   The Rite of Initiation into the Religious Life was seen as an act of embrace. For that rite the space should be configured around the candidate, who is welcomed into the community. The act of profession is more than a moment of reception. It is a ritual that announces advancement in the religious vocation and a commitment by the community. Consequently, those making profession are more prominent in this ceremony. The space should allow the candidate to be called forth from the community and to move to the chair. At the chair the candidate should profess vows into the hands of the seated superior.

In conclusion, temporary profession is very much like a celebration of Advent. Advent is a time of joyful expectation in which we recall what has been and look forward to what will be.[30] Temporary profession is similar. It celebrates the achievement of first stability and acceptance in the vowed community. It also looks forward to the completion of the journey in perpetual profession.

The Rite of Perpetual Profession

CONTEXT   This rite is the culmination of the initial formation process and the final act of incorporation into the religious community. Its significance is reflected in the dual instruction that the rites should take place on a Sunday or other significant feast[31] and that the faithful should be well informed of the time so that they can attend in greater number.[32] The level of festivity has no parallel in the other rites of profession.

Structurally, this ritual appears as an elaboration of the rite of temporary profession. During the eucharist, the rite unfolds after the gospel:

> call/request
> homily
> examination
> litany
> profession
> solemn blessing/consecration
> presentation of insignia
> [conclusion]

The basic difference between this outline and the one for temporary profession is the litany and solemn blessing that flank the profession of vows. Setting off the vows with such intercession and blessing highlights the central place of the profession of vows in this liturgy. The rest of the eucharist should enjoy a proportionate elaboration.

TEXTS   The opening prayers for the ritual Mass of perpetual profession have a distinctive baptismal flavor.[33] This imagery is echoed in the preface[34] and the intercessions of Eucharistic Prayer IV for men.[35] These texts offer valuable insights into the baptismal nature of these rites.[36]

MINISTRIES   Perpetual profession presumes a significant journey in faith and community growth for the candidate. Numerous people who contributed to the candidate's development will be in attendance. Some of them should be prominent in the various ministries of this liturgy. Such prominence suggests not only that they be seen but also that they be heard in the ritual. The call, for example, belongs to the director of formation who should also offer some testimony to the candidate's readiness for perpetual profession.[37] This personalization of the ministries should not devolve into the shaping of ministries according to the criterion of friendship. Rather, ministries should be shaped in view of the ecclesial and individual nature of this worship. Finally, the rite's preference for a concelebrated eucharist,[38] should be interpreted as a desire for ample solemnization of these rites. Concelebration itself may not be the most appropriate means for achieving this solemnization.

MUSIC Special liturgies are often marked by an elaborate musical program. Frequently, secondary elements receive the added musical attention in these situations while the primary elements are neglected. Whatever can be done to highlight the profession of vows should be done. This can be achieved by employing variations of the same music for the entire rite, which will contribute to the unity of these rites. Such variation on a musical theme—for example, by using the same music with different texts for the processional and recessional—will contribute to the unity and accessibility of the rite.

The Rite for Renewal of Vows

Though this rite will be discussed more thoroughly in the next chapter, it is appropriate to offer a few words of commentary on its structure and content here.

CONTEXT The introduction to this rite directs that the renewal of vows "should be conducted with the greatest simplicity, especially if . . . vows are renewed frequently or annually."[39] These rites might be compared to the special services of anointing for catechumens who mark their journey toward full initiation.[40] Thus, they are interim rituals that stand between first acceptance and definitive incorporation. Their simplicity should be maintained. At the same time we need to respect their significance in the journey toward perpetual profession. Often the renewal of vows is a time for considerable discernment and recommitment, so it should not be haphazardly planned or celebrated.

CENTRAL RITE   The rite, which may take place during Mass, consists of a prayer for God's grace and the renewal of vows. This ritual must be simple, but the current rite is underdeveloped. A modest elaboration of the rite, still respecting the transitional nature of the event, could better express the significance of the renewal.[41] This would also be a more appropriate ritual antecedent to perpetual profession.

Notes

1. MCW, n. 7.

2. One of the best of these is Austin Fleming, *Preparing for Liturgy: A Theology and Spirituality* (Washington, D.C.: Pastoral Press, 1985). Fleming's central message is that liturgies cannot be planned—for the tradition has already done that—but they need to be prepared (31).
     Also useful are Yvonne Cassa and Joanne Sanders, *Groundwork: Planning Liturgical Seasons* (Chicago: Liturgy Training Publications, 1982); *National Bulletin on Liturgy*, "Planning Our Year of Worship," 12 (1979), 3–32; Gil Ostdiek, *Catechesis for Liturgy* (Washington D.C.: Pastoral Press, 1986), 23–56; and Mark Searle, *Liturgy Made Simple* (Collegeville: Liturgical Press, 1981), 75–94.

3. For a discussion of primary and secondary elements within the context of the eucharistic prayer, see "Au cours des derniers mois," *Notitiae* 4 (1968), 148–55 (DOL, n. 1947).

4. "Since each of these rites has its own special character, each demands a celebration of its own." RRP, Introduction, n. 8.

5. For an example of such an introductory rite, see chapter 5.

6. MCW, n. 21.

7. GIRM, n. 58.

8. EACW, nn. 28-32.

9. This is the preference of CSL, n. 10.

10. Bishops' Committee on Priesthood, Life and Ministry, *Fulfilled in Your Hearing: The Homily in the Sunday Assembly* (Washington, D.C.: National Conference of Catholic Bishops, 1982), 17.

11. GIRM, n. 54.

12. For example, "Veni, Sancte Spiritus" by Jacques Berthier in *Music from Taizé* (Chicago: GIA Publications, Inc., 1981).

13. See EACW, nn. 49–51.

14. EACW, n. 53.

15. EACW, especially nn. 18–23, and 84–103.

16. For men, RRP 1:47; for women, RRP 2:52.

17. EACW, nn. 18–23.

18. Margaret Mead speaks of the ritual "guarantee" in "Ritual and Social Crisis," *The Roots of Ritual*, ed. James Shaughnessy (Grand Rapids: Eerdmans Publishing, 1973), 92.

19. For men, RRP 1:3; for women, RRP 2:3.

20. For men, RRP 1:2; for women, RRP 2:2.

21. For men, RRP 1:12; for women, RRP 2:12.

22. For men, RRP 1:4; for women, RRP 2:4.

23. For men, RRP 1:8; for women, RRP 2:8.

24. For men, RRP 1:5; for women, RRP 2:5.

25. For an introduction to the history and theology of temporary profession, see below, 104–5

26. For women, RRP 2:34.

27. For women, RRP 2:34; for men, RRP 1:31.

28. See RRP chapter 2, nn. 36, 43, 46, 53, 54 and 85.

29. For example, the litany of all saints and the prayer of consecration.

30. *General Norms for the Liturgical Year and the Calendar*, n. 39.

31. For men, RRP 1:40; for women, RRP 2:43.

32. For men, RRP 1:42; for women, RRP 2:45.

33. This is true of options A (206) and B (209–10).

34. ". . . consecrate more closely to your service those who leave all things for your sake," 213.

35. "Remember these our brothers who unite themselves more closely to you today by their perpetual profession," 207. Compare this with the parallel text for women: "Remember our sisters who have consecrated themselves to you today," 208.

36. For an example of how to emphasize the baptismal aspect of perpetual profession, see the ritual model in chapter 5.

37. For an example of how this might be done, see 104.

38. For men, RRP 1:44; for women, RRP 2:47.

39. For men, RRP 1:79; for women, RRP 2:86.
40. RCIA, nn. 98–103.
41. For an example of such elaboration, see chapter 5.

Ritual Models

S uggesting models for public ritual is a hazardous exercise for a number of reasons. First, ritual is something done by real people in ordinary or extraordinary circumstances. Author and reader do not have such circumstances in common; thus, the ritual models proposed here are offered in the abstract. Such abstraction may render these rituals accessible to large numbers of people in varying situations, but it cannot provide the individuality that makes a ritual a living event. A further difficulty stems from the fact that ritual is not something found in a book nor is it essentially a verbal enterprise. Yet words are all we have in this medium. Consequently, we are able to sketch only the basic shape of the ritual events and some of the accompanying processes. Even so, it is hoped that these rituals will be perceived not only in terms of their texts but also in terms of the gestures, music and ministry that give them life.

Despite these dangers, the presentation of ritual models has the advantage of offering at least a skeletal embodiment of the theory presented in the previous chapters. These narratives should be respected for what they are: abstract models that need to be adapted by the reader, schematic summaries, offered for reflection and adaptation. More important than any specific ritual formula are the underlying insights and principles.

The following outlines will occasionally require a reference to a religious community, founder, patron saint, etc. For the sake of explication, the examples will be drawn from my own community's tradition but will be set off in brackets to indicate their function as examples. This will also draw attention to one more instance where adaptation is required.

Because perpetual profession is the goal of initial formation and the ritual denouement of initiation into religious life, we will begin with specific reflections on the shaping of that ritual. We will turn then to the more difficult situation of the renewal of vows. The unusual nature of temporary profession will require some historical introduction, after which we will attempt to address not just the act of renewing vows but the broader evaluative processes that usually accompany this renewal. This will allow us to illustrate how the various stages of initiation into religious life must be integrated with the rituals that punctuate those stages.

Perpetual Profession

In our previous discussions of the rites of profession, we noted that the liturgy of perpetual profession requires a certain level of ritual inclusivity to engage the whole assembly. This inclusivity underscores the ecclesial nature of this event, stressing that profession is an act of the whole church, represented by the whole assembly.

One example of such ritual inclusivity entails the employment of the profession of faith from the church's Easter liturgy. This profession of faith can be used as an introductory rite for the whole assembly, followed by the call of the candidates, modulated within the broader profession of faith. The sprinkling rite follows as a confirmation of the community's faith and the call of the profession candidates:

INTRODUCTION

After the sign of the cross and greeting, the presider welcomes the assembly to a celebration that belongs to all. Profession is achieved in radical conformity with the baptismal commitment that transforms all of us in Christ. To enter appropriately into this celebration, therefore, requires the baptismal rededication of all in creed, water and prayer.

PROFESSION OF FAITH

Presider:

So I ask all of you who are baptized in Christ, do you believe in God, the Father almighty, creator of heaven and earth?

Assembly:

I do.

Presider:

Do you believe in Jesus Christ, his only son our Lord, who was born of the virgin Mary, was crucified, died and was buried, rose from the dead, and is now seated at the right hand of the Father?

Assembly:

I do.

Presider:

Do you believe in the Holy Spirit, the holy Catholic church, the communion of saints, the forgiveness of sins, the resurrection of the body, and life everlasting?

Assembly:

I do.

EXAMINATION OF CANDIDATES

Presider to the candidates:

You already have been consecrated to the Lord through baptism and therein have found the promise of eternal life. What further do you ask this day of the Lord and the church?

Candidates:

We are firm in our baptismal faith and know that it is the way to eternal life. We ask today that we might be allowed to live out this baptismal commitment as [Capuchins] and so give glory to God and serve the church for the rest of our lives.

Assembly:

Thanks be to God.

SPRINKLING RITE:

Acolytes bring water and bowl.

Presider:

Let us bless God who has given us this faith and who confirms our commitment in these baptismal waters.

Holy and eternal God, we give you thanks for our creation and redemption symbolized in this living water. We bless you for this holy sign that brings life and freshness to the earth, washes away our sins and inaugurates us into the way of eternal life.

With gratitude for your fidelity surpassing every hope, we ask you to send your living Spirit upon this water and upon those present who have already found rebirth in the font of your love. Renew the living spring of your life especially in our [sisters/brothers, N.], who this day offer themselves to you with a willing and joyful spirit.

Create in us a new heart and enliven us with zeal for your house. Fortify us with your word, so that we may reject all that is evil and embrace the way of your Son. Let his charity be our mission, his poverty our strength, his obedience to your will our promise of eternal life.

We make this and every prayer in the strong name of Jesus who is our hope and our joy, now and for ever. Amen.

Presider sprinkles the assembly.

OPENING PRAYER

Let us pray. Holy and eternal God, you are the source of every gift. We rightly praise you for the wonders you have wrought in your people and the faith you have given to your church. May those who consecrate themselves to you this day give voice to the promise of all the baptized and in turn be a sign of your blessing to all believers. May their consecration be a promise of your kingdom, revealed in Christ, who lives and reigns with you and the Holy Spirit, one God for ever and ever. Amen.

These introductory rites, which include the optional rite for calling the candidates,[1] accomplishes three important things. First, it situates the profession within a baptismal context, evoking and confirming the faith of the whole community. At the same time, the rite acknowledges the distinctive call of those to be professed, a call that specifies the baptismal call through the living of the evangelical counsels within a specific community. Finally, this adaptation allows the candidates to be actively engaged in this ritual event. They are called upon to speak and act in light of the profession they are about to make.

The actual profession of vows takes place after the gospel and traditionally consists of the call or request, the homily, the examination, the litany, the profession, the solemn blessing and the presentation of the insignia of profession. The call or request is an optional element more effectively employed within the introductory rites. The elimination of the call from the profession proper has the advantage of allowing the gospel and homily to operate as a single liturgical unit.

It might be effective to begin the examination with an invitation to profession. This would include a testimony to the readiness of the candidates by one who had a significant role in their formation. In place of a question-answer examination, during which the candidates simply respond "Amen," this invitation-testimony could be followed by a prepared statement by each candidate, addressing the fundamental issues of commitment, prayer and service. These are at the heart of the question-answer examination found in the ritual and need to be publicly articulated before the profession of vows.

INVITATION TO PROFESSION

Formation representative:

My [brothers], this day you have renewed your baptismal commitment, listened to the word of God, and attended to the challenge of this community. As one who has walked with you during this formative time, I can attest to your willingness to follow in the footsteps of [Francis], strive for holiness, serve your [brothers] and the whole people of God and embrace the gospel life. Before committing yourselves to our way of life perpetually, I ask you, in the presence of this community and almighty God, to speak again your willingness to live forever as a [Capuchin].

> *Each candidate speaks a few sentences that succinctly articulate their past experiences of community life in service and in holiness, their willingness to live this vowed life for the rest of their days and their affirmation that they will conform to the gospel and rule in a spirit of prayer at the service of the church.*

> *Presider:*

May God who has begun this good work in you bring it to fulfillment before the day of Christ Jesus. Amen.

> *The litany, profession, prayer of consecration and giving of insignia follow.*

Scrutinies during the Time of Temporary Profession

One of the most anomalous features of the initiatory process into religious life is the existence of temporary profession.[2] Most founders of religious communities did not foresee a period of testing after profession. Candidates made perpetual profession after the completion of novitiate. After the Council of Trent, however, some began to question the wisdom of this process. Such questioning found a receptive hearing by Pius IX (d. 1878), who feared that too many unworthy candidates were entering religious life. Consequently, in 1857 he decreed that after novitiate, candidates for solemn vows in men's communities were required to be in temporary vows for three years.[3]

The existence of temporary profession—which is sometimes characterized as permanent for the individual but temporary for the community—means that in most communities today there exists a period of probation after profession.[4] In one sense, there is no parallel here with initiation into the Christian community. Though the RCIA, for example, presumes a period of mystagogy or instruction after baptism, it does not consider the neophytes probationary. Those in temporary vows are not considered full members of the community and are constrained by certain canonical and formational restrictions. In some respects, those in temporary vows are like those who are chosen at the beginning of Lent for full initiation at Easter.

The ambiguous nature of temporary profession is seen most clearly in the ritual for the renewal of vows. This rite is underdeveloped to the point of being virtually nonexistent. Given the energy expended in the yearly discernments that lead to this renewal, however, and the high anxiety often generated among candidates and formation personnel throughout the accompanying evaluation processes, it is unfortunate that the rite of renewal is so sparse.

Given the similarities in status between catechumens who have been elected to full initiation and those in temporary profession, it might be effective to employ the characteristic ritual of the elect in their preparation before initiation: the scrutiny. As described in the RCIA, scrutinies

> are meant to uncover then heal all that is weak, defective, or sinful in the hearts of the elect; to bring out, then strengthen all that is upright, strong and good. For the scrutinies are celebrated in order to deliver the elect from the power of sin and Satan, to protect them against temptation, and to give them strength in Christ, who is the way, the truth, and the life. These rites, therefore, should complete the conversion of the elect and deepen their resolve to hold fast to Christ and to carry out their decision to love God above all.[5]

Traditionally occurring after the homily on the Third, Fourth and Fifth Sundays of Lent, scrutinies consist of silent prayer, a litany for the elect, prayer of exorcism, laying on of hands, prayer of blessing and dismissal of the elect. Scrutinies are not isolated rituals, but public moments of prayer integrated with the journey of the elect.

Those in temporary vows are likewise engaged on the journey toward full initiation into the community and could be similarly served by scrutiny rituals. For these to be effective, such scrutinies would have to be integrated into the processes that lead to the renewal of vows. For many simply professed, the movement toward renewal involves both their own personal discernment, accomplished with a spiritual mentor or director, and the more public discernment or evaluation of the community. A scrutiny rite could be a part of both stages. The ritual outline given here is conceived in terms of a public evaluation. Ritual principles and elements could easily be incorporated into personal discernment and direction. These are: 1) evaluation should take place in the context of prayer; 2) both exorcism and blessing, prayers of purification and those of strengthening are valuable; 3) these prayers should employ a combination of silent prayer, verbal prayer and ritual gesture.

This ritual presumes a time of shared evaluation. The scrutiny is meant to support that evaluation and to be the bridge between the evaluation and the renewal of vows. The scrutiny begins with a brief introduction, followed by silent prayer, a litany of intercession and a prayer of exorcism. The shared evaluation of the candidates follows; it presumably occurs as a dialogue. After the evaluation of the candidates there is a laying on of hands in silence, a prayer of blessing and the sign of peace.

INTRODUCTION

> *The superior of the community, the individual responsible for the formation of the candidates or some other appropriate person reminds the community that this scrutiny is both an act of worship and a gesture of charity. It is not only appropriate but necessary to offer prayer at this time of discernment, so that this is not merely the act of flawed human beings, but also an event of the Spirit. Then the community is invited into silent prayer.*

LITANY

Presider:

Let us together pray for the gift of the Holy Spirit in this moment of discernment, that our community might be strengthened and God praised through our sharing and prayer.

Cantor:

That those who take part in this evaluation might be graced with wisdom and understanding, let us pray to the Lord.

All:

Lord, hear our prayer.

Cantor:

That these candidates for the renewal of vows might be firm in their baptismal commitment and open to the challenge of this community, let us pray to the Lord.

All:

Lord, hear our prayer.

Cantor:

That these [brothers/sisters] might humbly accept their virtue and willingly acknowledge their sinfulness, let us pray to the Lord.

All:

Lord, hear our prayer.

Cantor:

That these [brothers/sisters] might grow in a spirit of prayer and daily advance in holiness, let us pray to the Lord.

All:

Lord, hear our prayer.

Cantor:

That this moment might enable them to discern God's call to them more clearly, let us pray to the Lord.

All:

Lord, hear our prayer.

Cantor:

That those who share their evaluations might do so in a spirit of charity and respect, let us pray to the Lord.

All:

Lord, hear our prayer.

Cantor:

That this gesture of love might serve to strengthen our community and to build up the whole body of Christ, let us pray to the Lord.

All:

Lord, hear our prayer.

EXORCISM

Presider:

Let us pray. Almighty and ever living God, in your loving kindness you sent your only Son among us, strong in goodness. Confident of your care and firm in our faith, we ask you to renew in our [brothers/sisters] the hope won by Christ's death and resurrection. Strengthen them to reject every vice and strive after every virtue. Give them a spirit of wisdom to accept what is true in the concerns shared with them. In this and every moment, keep them from self reliance and lead them to know your strength alone. So graced with new hearts and enlivened spirits, may they advance on the way to salvation. We ask this through Christ, who is Lord for ever and ever. Amen.

EVALUATION

The evaluation of all the candidates follows.

LAYING ON OF HANDS

After the evaluation, the candidates are asked to kneel and hands are laid upon them in silence. This can be done by the whole community or the community's representatives.

BLESSING

Presider:

God of every blessing, source of all that is good, we give you thanks for the wonders you have begun in us and the promises yet to be realized. We especially praise you for the calling that has moved our [brothers/sisters] and for their willingness to hear your voice and offer you their wholehearted response. Bless them with fortitude and perseverance that they might never abandon your invitation to holiness. Give them wisdom and understanding that they might come to know their place among your holy people. Fill them with the confidence that comes only from your presence and the charity that knows no bounds. May they dedicate themselves ever more fully to the mission of your Son and so be conformed to Christ who is Lord for ever and ever. Amen.

Sign of Peace

This scrutiny structure might also be employed in the renewal of vows that would occur after the evaluation process. If the renewal occurs during the eucharist, then the call to prayer, the litany and the exorcism would follow the gospel and homily. The laying on of hands, which linked the exorcism and blessing in the evaluation scrutiny, would be replaced by the ritual renewal of vows into the hands of the superior. The prayer of blessing and the sign of peace would follow. Though some further adaptations of the text might be necessary to employ this structure for the actual renewal of vows, the proposed scrutiny could enrich this otherwise feeble rite and offer strong ritual continuity between the evaluation process and the renewal itself.

Summary

As Austin Fleming has said, the task of those involved in the shaping of worship today is less one of planning than one of preparing. Fleming reminds us that, by the very nature of liturgy, much has already been done and many resources are already available. The task, therefore, is not essentially to devise or invent new liturgies, but to prepare as well as possible that worship that makes us the church.[6]

We have not attempted to invent new rituals in these pages but have appropriated and adapted already existing prayer forms for final profession and the renewal of vows. In so doing, we implicitly acknowledge that the church's traditional repertory of rituals is a treasury to be studied and respected. This does not mean that the contemporary experience has nothing to add to this treasury. On the contrary, the radical reform of our rites in the past two decades demonstrates just how much the 20th century has to contribute to the church's ritual vocabulary.

In this work, religious communities invite those who seek full initiation to steep themselves in the rituals that shaped these very communities. In doing so, we hand on what was entrusted to us and encourage women and men of vision to join us in professing our way of life.

Notes

1. RRP Introduction, n. 6.

2. For a discussion of the nature of temporary vows, see A. de Bonhome, "Voeux temporaires ou promesse temporaire?" *Vie consecré* 41 (1969), 239–42; J. M. Fisch, "Voeux temporaires ou promesse temporaire?" *Vie consecré* 41 (1969), 305–7; J. Gallen, "Temporary commitment to religious life," *Review for Religious* 33 (1974), 476–77; and A. Gutierrez, "Profession temporal sin intencion de perseverar?" *Sacra Congregatio pro Religiosis et Institutis Saecularibus Informationes* (1977), 73–79.

3. "Neminem latet," in *Collectanea in usum Secretariae Sacrae Congregationis Episcoporum et Regularium edita*, 2nd ed., by Andreas Bizzari (Rome: Polyglotta S. C. de Propaganda Fide, 1885), 853–54.

4. For a discussion of the contemporary law governing temporary profession (canons 655–57), see Rose M. McDermott, "Religious Profession," in *The Code of Canon Law: A Text and Commentary*, eds. James Coriden, Thomas Green and Donald Heintschel (New York: Paulist Press, 1985), 496–97.

5. RCIA, n. 141.

6. Fleming, *Preparing for Liturgy*, especially 31–41.

Appendix

THE ROMAN RITUAL

REVISED BY DECREE OF THE SECOND VATICAN ECUMENICAL
COUNCIL AND PUBLISHED BY AUTHORITY OF POPE PAUL VI

Rite of Religious Profession

Prepared by
International Commission on English in the Liturgy
A Joint Commission of Catholic Bishops' Conferences
and
Secretariat for the Liturgy
National Conference of Catholic Bishops

Foreword

On February 2, 1970 the Congregation for Divine Worship issued the Latin typical edition of *Ordo professionis religiosae.* An interim English translation was prepared by the International Commission on English in the Liturgy (ICEL) in 1971. A second revised edition was issued by ICEL in 1974.

On September 12, 1983 the Congregation for the Sacraments and Divine Worship published *Emendations in the Liturgical Books following upon the New Code of Canon Law.* This document indicates all the changes that are to be made in the liturgical books as a result of the promulgation of the revised *Code of Canon Law* of 1983. The most notable change made in the *Rite of Religious Profession* to conform it to the new *Code of Canon Law* is the deletion of the Rite of a Promise and of all references to it in the Introduction.

This revised edition of the *Rite of Religious Profession* contains all the changes mandated by the *Emendations,* as well as the 1982 revised translation of the Introduction to the rite, taken from *Documents on the Liturgy, 1963–1979: Conciliar, Papal, and Curial Texts.* In addition, the publication of this new edition has been the occasion to make several corrections in the text of the previous edition.

Secretariat for the Liturgy
National Conference of Catholic Bishops

SACRED CONGREGATION FOR DIVINE WORSHIP

Prot. n. 200/70

Decree

The rite of profession by which religious, in commitment to the evangelical counsels, vow themselves to God, has been revised in accord with the intent of the Constitution on the Liturgy. The life dedicated to God by the bonds of religious life has always held a place of high honor in the eyes of the Church, which from the earliest centuries has surrounded the act of religious profession with liturgical rites. The Fathers of Vatican Council II directed that a rite of religious profession and renewal of vows be drawn up that would contribute to greater unity, simplicity, and dignity and that, apart from exceptions in particular law, it should be adopted by those who make their profession or renewal of vows within Mass (art. 80).

Carrying out this directive, the Consilium has composed the present rite of religious profession; Pope Paul VI by his apostolic authority has approved it and ordered that it be incorporated into the Roman Ritual and published. Consequently this Congregation for Divine Worship, at the explicit mandate of the Pope, promulgates this rite.

The conferences of bishops (where applicable, through the joint commission of nations of the same language) are to see to the careful vernacular translations of the rite, after consultation with the conferences of major religious superiors in each country.

The rite of profession must be an expression of the identity and spirit of the individual religious family. Therefore each religious institute should adapt this rite in such a way that the ritual clearly brings out the institute's special character, then send the rite to this Congregation as soon as possible for confirmation.

All things to the contrary notwithstanding.

From the Sacred Congregation for Divine Worship, 2 February 1970, the feast of the Presentation of the Lord.

+ Benno Cardinal Gut, Prefect
A. Bugnini, Secretary

Introduction*

I. NATURE AND IMPORT OF RELIGIOUS PROFESSION

1.   In response to God's call many Christians dedicate themselves to his service and to the welfare of humanity through the sacred bonds of religious life and seek to follow Christ more closely through the evangelical counsels.[1] This leads to the grace of baptism achieving richer results in them.[2]

2.   The Church has always esteemed the religious life, which, under the guidance of the Holy Spirit, has taken various forms in the course of history.[3] It has raised religious life to the rank of a canonical state and approved a great number of religious institutes and protected them by wise legislation.[4]

    For it is the Church that receives the vows of those who make religious profession, begs God's grace for them by its public prayer, puts them in God's hands, blesses them, and unites their offering with the eucharistic sacrifice.[5]

II. Rites for the Different Stages of Religious Life

3.   The steps by which religious dedicate themselves to God and the Church are these: novitiate, first profession (or other sacred bonds), and final profession. The constitutions of religious institutes add to these a renewal of vows.

4.   The novitiate, the beginning of life in the institute,[6] is a time of testing for both novice and community. Entry into the novitiate should be marked by a rite in which God's grace is sought for the special purpose of the period. This rite should, of its nature, be restrained and simple, celebrated in the presence only of the religious community. It should take place outside Mass.

5.   First profession then follows. Through temporary vows made before God and the Church the novices promise to observe the evangelical counsels. Such vows may be taken within Mass, but without special solemnity. The rite of first profession provides for the bestowal of insignia of the religious life and the habit, following the very ancient custom of giving the habit at the end of the period of probation, since the habit is a sign of consecration.[7]

6.   After the period prescribed by law, final profession is made, by which religious bind themselves permanently to the service of God and the Church. Perpetual profession reflects the unbreakable union between Christ and his Bride, the Church.[8]

It is very fitting that the rite of final profession should take place within Mass, with due solemnity and in the presence of the religious community and the people.[9] The rite consists of these parts:

> a. the calling or asking of those to be professed (this may be omitted if desired);
> b. the homily or address, which reminds the people and those to be professed of the value of religious life;
> c. The examination by which the celebrant or superior asks those who are to be professed whether they are
> prepared to be consecrated to God and to follow the way of perfect charity, according to the rule of their religious family;
> d. the litanies, in which prayer is offered to God the Father and the intercession of the Blessed Virgin Mary and all the saints is invoked;

e. the profession, made in the presence of the Church, the lawful superior of the institute, the witnesses, and the congregation;

f. the solemn blessing or consecration of the professed, by which the Church ratifies their profession through a liturgical consecration, asking the heavenly Father to pour forth upon them the gifts of the Holy Spirit;

g. the presentation of the insignia of profession, if this is the custom of the religious family, as outward signs of perpetual dedication to God.

7.   In some religious communities vows are renewed at fixed times in accordance with the constitutions.

This renewal of vows may take place within Mass, but without solemnity, especially if renewal of vows is frequent or annual.

A liturgical rite has place only in the case of renewal of vows that has the force of law. In many religious communities, however, the custom of renewing vows has become established as an exercise of devotion. It may be carried out in many ways; but the practice of doing publicly within Mass what belongs to private devotion is not to be encouraged. If it seems appropriate to renew vows publicly on special anniversaries, for example, the twenty-fifth or fiftieth year of religious life, the rite for the renewal of vows may be used with the necessary adaptations.

8.   Since all these rites have their own special character, each demands a celebration of its own. The celebration of several rites within the same liturgical service is to be absolutely excluded.

III. Mass for the Rite of Religious Profession

9.   Whenever religious profession, and especially final profession, takes place within Mass, it is appropriate to choose one of the ritual Masses for the day of religious profession from the Roman Missal or from approved propers. In the case of a Sunday of Advent, Lent, or Easter, of any solemnity, or of Ash Wednesday and all of Holy Week, the Mass is that of the day; but the special formularies for the professed during the eucharistic prayer and the final blessing may be retained.

10.   Since the liturgy of the word for the rite of profession can be an important aid to bringing out the meaning of religious life and its responsibilities, it is lawful, when the Mass for the day of religious profession may not be used, to take one reading from the special list of readings for the rite of profession. But this may not be done during the Easter triduum, on the solemnities of Christmas, Epiphany, Ascension, Pentecost, or Corpus Christi, or on other solemnities of obligation.

11.   White vestments are worn for the ritual Mass for the day of religious profession.

IV. ADAPTATIONS TO BE MADE BY INDIVIDUAL INSTITUTES

12.   The norms governing the rite of initiation (nos. 1–13 of the ritual) are not of obligation unless this is clearly stated (as in the prohibition of having the rite within Mass, no. 2) or the nature of the rite so demands (as in the rule that the rite should be restrained and simple, no. 3).

13.   All who make or renew their religious profession within Mass must use the rites of temporary profession, final profession, or renewal of vows, unless they possess a particular right in this matter.[10]

14.   Religious families should adapt the rite so that it more clearly reflects and manifests the character and spirit of each institute. For this purpose the faculty of adapting the rite is given to each institute; its decisions are then to be reviewed by the Apostolic See.

In making adaptations in the rite of profession, the following points should be especially respected:

a. The rite must take place immediately after the gospel.

b. The arrangement of parts must remain intact, but some parts may be omitted or others of a similar nature substituted.

c. A liturgical distinction between perpetual profession and temporary profession or renewal of vows must be strictly maintained. What is proper to one rite may not be inserted into another.

d. As is stated in the pertinent places, many formularies in the rite of profession may be changed, and in fact must be, to reflect more clearly the character and spirit of each institute. Where the

Roman Ritual offers several optional formularies, particular rituals may add others of the same kind.

15.   Profession in the presence of the blessed sacrament, prior to communion, is not in harmony with a true understanding of the liturgy. Henceforth, then, new religious communities are forbidden to adopt the practice. Institutes that follow this practice on the basis of a particular law are urged to discontinue it.

Similarly, all religious following a rite proper to them are instructed to embrace and follow authentic liturgical forms, putting aside anything in conflict with the principles of the liturgical reform. This is the way to achieve that simplicity, dignity, and closer unity that the Council has so strongly endorsed.[11]

Notes

*The text here is based on the second printing, which carries the following note: "It is necessary to reprint the *Ordo professionis religiosae,* first published in 1970. Therefore it seemed advisable to provide this reprint with certain minor changes:

1. The texts of the psalms and of the New Testament have been taken from the Neo-Vulgate edition of the Bible.

2. There are some emendations of titles and rubrics in order that these might more closely correspond to the language and style found in the liturgical books published since 1969.

3. The liturgical texts can be adapted to fit particular situations by a change in gender or number.

1. See LG, no. 43; PC, no. 1.

2. See LG, no. 43.

3. See ibid.; PC, no. 1.

4. See LG, no. 45; PC, no. 1.

5. See LG, no. 45.

6. See CIC, can. 646.

7. See PC, no. 17.

8. See LG, no. 44.

9. See SC, art. 80.

10. See ibid.

11. See ibid.

PART I
Rite of Religious Profession for Men

CHAPTER I
Norms for the Rite of Initiation into the Religious Life

1.   On the day when the canonical novitiate begins, it is fitting that there should be a ceremony to ask God's grace for achieving the special purpose of the novitiate.

2.   It is forbidden to perform the rite of initiation during Mass.

3.   The rite is to be very simple and direct, in the presence of the religious community only.

4.   The texts for the rite must avoid anything that may seem to diminish the novices' freedom of choice or obscure the true meaning of a noviceship or time of testing.

5.   The chapter hall or other similar room is an appropriate setting for the rite. If it seems necessary, however, the rite may take place in the chapel.

OUTLINE OF THE RITE

INTRODUCTORY RITES
Greeting or Song
Questioning of the Postulants or Request for Admission
Opening Prayer

CELEBRATION OF THE WORD OF GOD

CONCLUDING RITES
General Intercessions
Lord's Prayer
Concluding Prayer

It is appropriate that the rite should take place during a special celebration of the word on the nature of the religious life and the spirit of the institute.

INTRODUCTORY RITES

GREETING OR SONG

6. *The rite may appropriately begin with a greeting by the superior, or the singing of a psalm or other suitable hymn.*

QUESTIONING OF THE POSTULANTS OR REQUEST FOR ADMISSION

7. *Then the superior questions the postulants in these or similar words:*

Dear sons (brothers), what do you ask from us?

The postulants reply together in these or similar words:

We wish to try your way of life,
and are willing to be tested ourselves,
that we may follow Christ wholeheartedly
in this community of N.

The superior replies:

May the Lord grant you his help.

R.   Amen.

8. *The questioning may be omitted, and the request for admission may take place as follows: one of the postulants, facing the superior and community, speaks in the name of all:*

Drawn by God's mercy,
we have come here to learn your way of life.
We ask you to teach us to follow Christ crucified
and to live in poverty, obedience and chastity.
Teach us to persevere in prayer and penance,
in the service of the Church and of humankind.
Teach us to be one with you in heart and mind.
Help us to live out the Gospel every day of our lives.
Teach us your rule and help us to learn to love
our brothers as Christ commanded us.

Or he may use similar words, expressing the aspirations and thoughts of the postulants themselves.

The superior responds in these or similar words:

May God in his mercy be with you always
and may Christ our teacher grant light to us all.

R.   Amen.

OPENING PRAYER

9.   *After the questioning or request for admission, the superior says:*

Let us pray.

Lord God, you give us the desire to hear your call.
Listen favorably to the prayers of your servants N. and N.,
who, desiring to serve you more perfectly,
ask to join our community.
Grant that our life in common
may become a communion of love.

We ask this through Christ our Lord.

R.   Amen.

CELEBRATION OF THE WORD OF GOD

10.   *Suitable texts from holy Scripture are then read, with appropriate responsories (see nos. 91–136).*

11.   *At their conclusion the superior addresses the religious community and the postulants on the meaning of the religious life and the spirit of the institute, or he reads an appropriate chapter of the rule.*

CONCLUDING RITES

12.   *The rite fittingly concludes with the general intercessions (prayer of the faithful) and the Lord's Prayer, to which a suitable prayer may be added, such as:*

Lord God,
you call us to your service
and inspire us to hear your call.
These brothers of ours
desire to test our way of life:
help them to know what you ask of them
and strengthen us all in your service.

We ask this through Christ our Lord.

R.   Amen.

> 13.   *After this the superior entrusts the newly admitted novices to the care of the novice master, and with his fellow religious greets them in the spirit of Christian love in the way customary in the religious community. Meanwhile, an appropriate song or a canticle of praise is sung.*

CHAPTER II
Rite of Temporary Profession During Mass

14.   The rite described in this chapter takes place during Mass. It may be used only for those religious who make their first profession upon successful completion of the novitiate (see Introduction, no. 5).

15.   The Mass may correspond to the liturgy of the day, or the ritual Mass for the day of first profession may be used, in accordance with the rubrics (see Introduction 9–11).

16.   In clerical institutes it is proper for the superior who receives the profession to preside over the eucharistic sacrifice. In lay institutes a chair should be prepared in a convenient part of the sanctuary for the superior who is to receive the profession of the members of the institute.

17.   The profession ordinarily takes place at the chair; if circumstances so dictate, the chair may be placed in front of the altar. Seats should be so arranged in the sanctuary for those making profession that the faithful have a complete view of the liturgical rites.

18.   Enough bread and wine for consecration should be prepared for the ministers, those making their profession, and their parents, relatives, and fellow religious. If only one chalice is used, it should be sufficiently large.

19.   In addition to what is needed for Mass, there should also be ready:

a) the ritual for religious profession;

b) the religious habit, if the religious institute has decided to present it on the occasion of first profession (see Introduction, no. 5);

c) the book of the rule or constitutions, and other insignia of religious profession which, according to law or custom, are to be presented.

OUTLINE OF THE RITE

INTRODUCTORY RITES
LITURGY OF THE WORD
RELIGIOUS PROFESSION
      Calling or Request
      Homily or Address
      Examination
      Prayer for God's Grace
      Profession
      Presentation of the Insignia of Religious Profession
         Presentation of the Religious Habit
         Presentation of the Rule or Constitutions
      General Intercessions
LITURGY OF THE EUCHARIST

INTRODUCTORY RITES

20.   *When the people and the religious are assembled and everything is ready, the procession moves through the church to the altar in the usual way, while the choir and people sing the entrance song of the Mass. Those to be professed may fittingly join in the procession, accompanied by the novice master and, in lay institutes, the superior.*

21.   *When they come to the sanctuary all make the customary reverence to the altar and go to their places; then Mass continues.*

LITURGY OF THE WORD

22.   *The liturgy of the word takes place as usual, except for the following:*

>   *a) the readings may be taken from the Mass of the day or from the texts in nos. 91–136 (see Introduction, nos. 9–10);*
>   *b) the profession of faith may be omitted, even if prescribed by the rubrics of the day.*

RELIGIOUS PROFESSION

CALLING OR REQUEST

23.   *After the gospel the celebrant and the people sit, but those to be professed stand. Then, according to choice or as circumstances demand, the deacon or the novice master calls those to be professed by name.*

They answer:

Present,

or they make some other reply according to local usage or the custom of the religious community.

24.   *The celebrant then questions them in these or similar words:*

My dear brothers (sons), what do you ask of God and of his holy Church?

The candidates reply together in these or similar words:

We ask for God's merciful love
and for the grace of serving him more perfectly
in your (this) religious community.

> *The celebrant and all the members of the religious community reply:*

Thanks be to God,

> *or they express their approval in some other way.*

---

25.   *The calling by name and the questioning by the celebrant may be omitted; a request by those to be professed may take their place. For example, one of those to be professed may stand facing the celebrant (or superior) and say, in the name of all, these or similar words:*

With the help of God,
we (N. and N.) have studied your rule
and have lived among you as your brothers for the time of probation.
Father (Brother), we now ask to be allowed
to dedicate ourselves to God and his kingdom
by making profession in this religious community of N.

> *The celebrant and all the members of the religious community reply:*

Thanks be to God,

> *or they express their approval in some other way.*

HOMILY OR ADDRESS

26.   *Those to be professed then sit and listen to the homily or address which should develop the scriptural readings and the theme of religious profession as God's gift and call for the sanctification of those chosen and for the good of the Church and the whole human family.*

EXAMINATION

27.   *After the homily or address, those to be professed stand, and the celebrant questions them on their readiness to dedicate themselves to God and to seek perfect charity, according to the rule or constitutions of the religious community. The questions may be changed or in part omitted, to suit the spirit and character of each religious institute.*

My dear sons (brothers),
by water and the Holy Spirit
you have already been consecrated to God's service:
are you resolved to unite yourselves more closely to him
by the new bond of religious profession?

They answer:

I am.

The celebrant continues:

In your desire to follow Christ perfectly,
are you resolved to live in chastity
for the sake of the kingdom of heaven,
to choose a life of poverty,
and to offer the sacrifice of obedience?

They answer:

I am.

28.   *Then the celebrant confirms their intention in these or similar words:*

May almighty God grant you his grace
to fulfill what you resolve.

R.   Amen.

PRAYER FOR GOD'S GRACE

29.   *The celebrant then prays for God's help, saying:*

Let us pray.

All pray for a while in silence. Then the celebrant says:

Lord,
look upon these servants of yours
who are resolved to dedicate their lives to you
by making profession of the evangelical counsels
in the presence of your Church today.
Mercifully grant that their manner of life
may bring glory to your name
and further your loving plan of redemption.

We ask this through Christ our Lord.

R.   Amen.

PROFESSION

30.   *After the prayer, if it is the custom of the religious community, two professed religious stand near the celebrant (or superior) to act as witnesses. Those to be professed come, one by one, to the celebrant and read the formula of profession.*

If there are very many religious making their profession, the formula of profession may be recited by all together. The concluding words, This I promise . . . *or the like, must be said by each individually as a clear expression of his will. Then they return to their places and remain standing.*

PRESENTATION OF THE INSIGNIA OF RELIGIOUS PROFESSION

PRESENTATION OF THE RELIGIOUS HABIT

31.   *After this the novice master and some members of the community present the religious habit to each of the newly professed to put on in the sanctuary or other suitable place. Meanwhile the choir may begin the antiphon:*

Lord, these are the men who long to see your face,
who seek the face of the God of Jacob (Psalm 24:6),

with Psalm 24; or some other appropriate song may be sung. The antiphon is repeated after every two verses; at the end of the psalm Glory to the Father *is not said but only the antiphon. If the presentation of the habits comes to an end before the whole psalm is sung, the psalm is interrupted and the antiphon repeated.*

PRESENTATION OF THE RULE OR CONSTITUTIONS

32.   *Then, if customary, the newly professed, wearing the religious habit, come to the celebrant (or superior) who gives each the book of the rule or constitutions, saying these or similar words:*

Receive the rule of our (this) religious community.
By keeping it faithfully, may you arrive at the perfection of love.

The professed replies:

Amen.

After receiving the book, he returns to his place and remains standing.

33.   *If the newly professed are numerous or there is some other reason, the celebrant (or superior) may present the rule and say the formula once only in these or similar words:*

Receive the rule of our (this) religious community.
By keeping it faithfully, may you arrive at the perfection of love.

The professed reply together:

Amen.

Then they come forward to the celebrant (superior) who gives each the book of the rule or constitutions. After receiving the book, they return to their places and remain standing.

34.   If, in accordance with the rules or customs of the religious community, other insignia of religious profession are to be presented, this is done now in silence or with a suitable formula. In this matter a dignified simplicity should be observed.

35.   An alternative way of presenting the insignia of profession is described in nos. 137–139.

GENERAL INTERCESSIONS

36.   The rite fittingly concludes with the general intercessions (prayer of the faithful). For these, the formula given in nos. 140–142 may be used.

LITURGY OF THE EUCHARIST

37.   During the offertory song, some of the newly professed religious may bring the bread, wine, and water to the altar for the eucharistic sacrifice.

38.   If it seems opportune, the celebrant gives the sign of peace to each of the newly professed religious in the usual way or in accordance with the customs of the religious community of the place.

39.   After the celebrant has received the body and blood of Christ, the newly professed religious come to the altar to receive communion, which may be given to them under both kinds. Then their parents, relatives, and fellow religious may receive communion in the same way.

CHAPTER III
Rite of Perpetual Profession During Mass

40. It is fitting that the rite of profession by which a religious binds himself to God for ever should take place on a Sunday or a solemnity of the Lord, of the Blessed Virgin Mary, or of a saint distinguished in the living of the religious life.

41. The rite of perpetual profession takes place separately from other rites of profession (see Introduction, no. 8).

42. Notice of the day and hour should be given to the faithful in good time so that they may attend in greater numbers.

43. The Mass is that of the liturgy of the day, or the ritual Mass for the day of perpetual religious profession may be used, in accordance with the rubrics (see Introduction, nos. 9–11).

44. Where possible and if the needs of the faithful do not demand individual celebration by the priests present, it is preferable that the Mass be concelebrated. If the superior who is to receive the profession is a priest, he should be the celebrant.

45. Profession ordinarily takes place in the church of the religious community. For pastoral reasons, however, or in order to promote esteem for the religious life, to give edification to the people of God, or to permit larger attendance, the rite may take place in the cathedral, parish church, or some other notable church, as may seem fitting.

46. Similarly, where religious from two or more institutes wish to celebrate their profession at the same eucharistic sacrifice, the rite of profession may suitably take place in the cathedral, a parish church, or some other notable church with the bishop presiding and the superiors of the institutes concelebrating. Those making their profession will pronounce their vows before their respective superiors.

47. As the nature of the rite demands, the whole liturgical service should be celebrated with fitting solemnity, but any appearance of lavishness unbecoming to religious poverty should be avoided.

48. The profession ordinarily takes place at the chair. To enable the faithful to take part more easily, the celebrant's chair may be placed in front of the altar. In lay institutes, a chair is to be prepared in a suitable

part of the sanctuary for the superior who is to receive the profession of the members of the institute. Seats should be so arranged in the sanctuary for those making profession that the faithful may have a complete view of the liturgical rites.

49.   Enough bread and wine for consecration should be prepared for the ministers, those making their profession, and their parents, relatives, and fellow religious. If only one chalice is used, it should be sufficiently large.

50.   In addition to what is needed for Mass, there should also be ready:

a) the ritual for religious profession;
b) the insignia of religious profession, if these are to be presented in accordance with the rules or customs of the religious community.

OUTLINE OF THE RITE

INTRODUCTORY RITES
LITURGY OF THE WORD
RELIGIOUS PROFESSION
Calling or Request
Homily or Address
Examination
Litany
Profession
Solemn Blessing or Consecration of the Professed
Presentation of the Insignia of Profession
Statement of Admission or Sign of Peace
LITURGY OF THE EUCHARIST
CONCLUDING RITE
Solemn Blessing

INTRODUCTORY RITES

51.   *When the people and the religious are assembled and everything is ready, the procession moves through the church to the altar in the usual way, while the choir and people sing the entrance song of the Mass. Those to be professed may fittingly join in the procession, accompanied by the novice master and, in lay institutes, the superior. When they come to the sanctuary, all make the customary reverence to the altar and go their places; then Mass continues.*

LITURGY OF THE WORD

52.   *The liturgy of the word takes place as usual, except for the following:*

a) the readings may be taken from the Mass of the day or from the texts in nos. 91–136 (see Introduction, nos. 9–10);
b) the profession of faith may be omitted, even if prescribed by the rubrics of the day.
c) the general intercessions in the form customarily used during the celebration of Mass are omitted (see no. 62).

RELIGIOUS PROFESSION

CALLING OR REQUEST

53.   *After the gospel the celebrant and the people sit, but those to be professed stand. Then, according to choice or as circumstances demand, the deacon or the novice master calls those to be professed by name.*

They answer:

Present,

or they make some other reply according to local usage or the custom of the religious community.

54.   *The celebrant then questions them in these or similar words:*

My dear brothers (sons), what do you ask of God and of his holy Church?

The candidates reply together in these or similar words:

We ask for perseverance in God's service
and in your religious community
all the days of our lives.

The celebrant and all the members of the religious community reply:

Thanks be to God,

or they express their approval in some other way.

---

55.   *The calling by name and the questioning by the celebrant may be omitted; a request by those to be professed may take their place. For example, one of those to be professed may stand facing the celebrant (or superior) and say, in the name of all, these or similar words:*

With the help of God,
we (N. and N.) have come to know
the life of religious dedication in your community.
Father (Brother), we now ask to be allowed
to make perpetual profession in this religious community of N.
for the glory of God and the service of the Church.

The celebrant and all the members of the religious community reply:

Thanks be to God,

or they express their approval in some other way.

HOMILY OR ADDRESS

56.   *Those to be professed then sit and listen to the homily or address which should develop the scriptural readings and the theme of religious profession as God's gift and call for the sanctification of those chosen and for the good of the Church and the whole human family.*

EXAMINATION

57.   *After the homily or address, those to be professed stand, and the celebrant questions them on their readiness to dedicate themselves to God and to seek perfect charity, according to the rule or constitutions of the religious community. The questions may be changed or in part omitted, to suit the spirit and character of each religious institute.*

The celebrant questions them, saying:

Dear sons (brothers),
in baptism you have already died to sin
and been consecrated to God's service.
Are you now resolved to unite yourself more closely to God
by the bond of perpetual profession?

They answer:

I am.

The celebrant continues:

Are you resolved,
with the help of God,
to undertake that life of perfect chastity, obedience, and poverty
chosen for themselves by Christ our Lord and his Virgin Mother,
and to persevere in it for ever?

They answer:

I am.

The celebrant continues:

Are you resolved to strive steadfastly for perfection
in the love of God and of your neighbor
by living the Gospel with all your heart
and keeping the rule of the religious community?

They answer:

I am.

The celebrant continues:

Are you resolved,
with the help of the Holy Spirit,
to spend your whole life in the generous service of God's people?

They answer:

I am.

58.   *In the case of religious communities wholly dedicated to the
contemplative life, this may appropriately be added:*

The celebrant asks:

Are you resolved to live for God alone,
in solitude and silence,
in persevering prayer and willing penance,
in humble work and holiness of life?

>*They answer:*

I am.

>*59. At the end of the questions, the celebrant confirms the intention of those to be professed in these or similar words:*

May God who has begun the good work in you
bring it to fulfillment
before the day of Christ Jesus.

>*All:*

Amen.

LITANY

>*60. All then rise. The celebrant stands with hands joined and says, facing the people:*

Dear friends in Christ,
let us pray to God the almighty Father
for these servants of his
whom he has called to follow Christ in the religious life;
in his love may he bless them with his grace
and strengthen them in their holy purpose.

>*61. The deacon gives the sign to kneel.*

Let us kneel.

>*The celebrant kneels at his chair. Those to be professed prostrate themselves or kneel, according to the custom of the place or of the religious community. The rest kneel. During the Easter Season and on all Sundays, all stand except those to be professed.*

>*62. Then the cantors sing the litany for the rite of religious profession, all making the responses. In this litany one or other of the petitions marked with the same letter may be omitted. At the appropriate place there may be inserted invocations of saints especially venerated in the religious community or by the faithful; other petitions may be added to suit the occasion.*

Lord, have mercy	Lord, have mercy
Christ, have mercy	Christ, have mercy
Lord, have mercy	Lord, have mercy
Holy Mary, Mother of God	pray for us
Saint Michael	pray for us
Holy angels of God	pray for us
Saint John the Baptist	pray for us
Saint Joseph	pray for us
Saint Peter and Saint Paul	pray for us
Saint John	pray for us
Saint Mary Magdalene	pray for us
Saint Stephen and Saint Lawrence	pray for us
Saint Agnes	pray for us
Saint Basil	pray for us
Saint Augustine	pray for us
Saint Benedict	pray for us
Saint Bernard	pray for us
Saint Francis and Saint Dominic	pray for us
Saint Ignatius of Loyola	pray for us
Saint Vincent de Paul	pray for us
Saint John Bosco	pray for us
Saint Catherine of Siena	pray for us
Saint Teresa of Jesus	pray for us
All holy men and women	pray for us
Lord, be merciful	Lord, save your people
From all evil	Lord, save your people
From every sin	Lord, save your people
From everlasting death	Lord, save your people
By your coming as man	Lord, save your people
By your death and rising to new life	Lord, save your people
By your gift of the Holy Spirit	Lord, save your people
Be merciful to us sinners	Lord, hear our prayer

a) By the self-offering of your servants
and their apostolic work,
make the life of your Church
ever more fruitful.
Lord, hear our prayer

a) Give in ever greater abundance
the gifts of the Holy Spirit
to your servant, Pope N.,
and to all his brother bishops.   Lord, hear our prayer

b) By the life and labor of all religious
promote the welfare of all people.   Lord, hear our prayer

b) Lead all men and women
to the fullness of the Christian life.   Lord, hear our prayer

c) Grant that all religious communities
may live and grow
in the love of Christ
and the spirit of their founders.   Lord, hear our prayer

c) Give to all
who profess the Gospel counsels
a fuller share in the work of redemption.   Lord, hear our prayer

d) Reward a hundredfold
the parents of your servants
for the sacrifice they have made.   Lord, hear our prayer

e) Make these servants of yours
more and more like Christ,
the firstborn among many.   Lord, hear our prayer

e) Give these servants of yours
the grace of perseverance.   Lord, hear our prayer

e) Bless these brothers of ours,
your servants,
make them holy,
and consecrate them to your service.   Lord, hear our prayer

Jesus, Son of the living God   Lord, hear our prayer
Christ, hear us   Christ, hear us
Lord Jesus, hear our prayer   Lord Jesus, hear our prayer

63. *Then the celebrant alone rises and says, with hands joined:*

Lord,
grant the prayers of your people.
Prepare the hearts of your servants
for consecration to your service.

By the grace of the Holy Spirit,
purify them from all sin
and set them on fire with your love.

We ask this through Christ our Lord.

R.   Amen.

The deacon then says:

Let us rise.

All stand.

PROFESSION

64.   *After the litany, if it is the custom of the religious community,
two professed religious stand near the chair of the celebrant (or
superior) to act as witnesses. Those to be professed come, one by one, to
the celebrant (or superior) and read the formula of profession, which
they themselves have written out beforehand.*

65.   *Then the newly professed may fittingly go to the altar, one by
one, to place on it the formula of profession; if it can be done conve-
niently, each of them should sign the document of profession upon the
altar itself. After this, each goes back to his place.*

66.   *Afterward, if this is the practice of the community, the newly
professed may stand and sing an antiphon or other song expressing the
spirit of self-giving and joy, for example:*

Uphold me, Lord, according to your promise
and I shall live;
and do not bring to nothing all my hope (Psalm 119:116).

SOLEMN BLESSING OR CONSECRATION OF THE PROFESSED

67.   *Then the newly professed kneel; the celebrant, with hands
extended over them, says the prayer of blessing* Father in heaven,
source of all holiness, *in which the words in parentheses may, to suit
the occasion, be omitted, or else the prayer* Lord God, source of holiness
and growth in your Church, *which is found in no. 143.*

Father in heaven,
source of all holiness,
creator of the human race,
your love for us was so great
that you gave us a share in your own divine life.

Neither the sin of Adam
nor even the sins of the whole world
could alter your loving purpose.

In the dawn of history
you gave us Abel as an example of holiness.
Later, from your beloved Hebrew people
you raised up men and women graced with every virtue.

Foremost among them all stands Mary,
the ever-virgin daughter of Zion.
From her pure womb was born Jesus Christ,
your eternal Word,
the Savior of the world.

You sent him, Father, as our pattern of holiness.
He became poor to make us rich,
a slave to set us free.
With love no words can tell
he redeemed the world by his paschal mystery
and won from you the gifts of the Spirit
to sanctify his Church.

The voice of the Spirit has drawn
countless numbers of your children
to follow in the footsteps of your Son.
They leave all things
to be one with you in the bonds of love
and give themselves wholly to your service
and the service of all your people.

Look with favor, then,
on these who have heard your call.
Send them the Spirit of holiness;
help them to fulfill in faith
what you have enabled them to promise in joy.
Keep always before their eyes Christ, the divine teacher.

[Give them perfect chastity,
ungrudging poverty
and wholehearted obedience.
May they glorify you by their humility,
serve you with docility,
and be one with you in fervent love.]

May they build up the Church by the holiness of their lives,
advance the salvation of the world,
and stand as a sign of the blessings that are to come.

Lord, protect and guide these servants of yours.
At the judgment seat of your Son
be yourself their great reward.
Give them the joy of vows fulfilled.
Made perfect in your love,
may they rejoice in the communion of your saints
and praise you for ever in their company.

We ask this through Christ our Lord.

R.   Amen.

PRESENTATION OF THE INSIGNIA OF PROFESSION

68.   *After the blessing of the professed, if it is the custom of the religious community to present insignia of religious profession, the newly professed rise and come before the celebrant, who presents the insignia to each in silence or with a suitable formula.*

69.   *Meanwhile the choir and people together sing the antiphon:*

How happy, Lord, are those who dwell in your house,
who sing your praise for ever (Psalm 84:5),

with Psalm 84; or some other appropriate song may be sung. The antiphon is repeated after every two verses; at the end of the psalm Glory to the Father is not said but only the antiphon. If the presentation of the insignia comes to an end before the whole psalm is sung, the psalm is interrupted and the antiphon is repeated.

STATEMENT OF ADMISSION OR SIGN OF PEACE

70.   *When the presentation of the insignia is completed, or after the prayer of solemn blessing, if it is customary or seems opportune, there may be a ceremony to mark the fact that the newly professed religious have been admitted as lifelong members of the institute or religious family. This can take the form of a suitable statement by the celebrant (or superior) or the the sign of peace. For example:*

a) The celebrant (or superior) says these or similar words:

We confirm that you are now one with us
as members of this religious community of N.,

sharing all things in common with us
now and in the future.

He may add:
Be faithful to the ministry the Church entrusts to you
to be carried out in its name.

The members of the community manifest their assent, saying:

R.   Amen.

*b) The above may be omitted and the celebrant (or superior) and
members of the community may give the sign of peace to the newly
professed in the usual way or according to the custom of the place.
Meanwhile the choir and the people sing the antiphon:*

See how good it is, how pleasant,
that brothers live in unity (Psalm 133:1),

with Psalm 133; or some other appropriate song may be sung.

71.   *The newly professed religious return after this to their places. The
Mass continues.*

LITURGY OF THE EUCHARIST

72.   *During the offertory song, some of the newly professed may bring
to the altar the bread, wine, and water for the eucharistic sacrifice.*

73.   *In the eucharistic prayers, the offering of the professed may be
mentioned according to the texts below:*

a) In Eucharistic Prayer I, the special form of Father, accept this
offering *is said:*

Father, accept and sanctify this offering
from your whole family and from these your servants
which we make to you on the day of their profession.
By your grace
they have dedicated their lives to you today.
When your Son returns in glory,
may they share the joy of the unending paschal feast.

[Through Christ our Lord. Amen.]

b) In the intercessions of Eucharistic Prayer II, after the words and all
the clergy, *there is added:*

Lord, remember also these our brothers
who have today dedicated themselves to serve you always.
Grant that they may always raise their minds and hearts to you
and glorify your name.

> *c) In the intercessions of Eucharistic Prayer III, after the words* your
> Son has gained for you, *there is added:*

Strengthen also these your servants in their holy purpose,
for they have dedicated themselves
by the bonds of religious consecration to serve you always.
Grant that they may give witness in your Church
to the new and eternal life won by Christ's redemption.

> *d) In the intercessions of Eucharistic Prayer IV, the professed may be
> mentioned in this way:*

. . . bishop, and bishops and clergy everywhere.
Remember these our brothers
who unite themselves more closely to you today
by their perpetual profession.
Remember those who take part in this offering . . .

> 74.   *The celebrant gives the sign of peace to each of the newly
> professed in the usual way, or according to the custom of the place or of
> the religious community.*

> 75.   *After the celebrant has received the body and blood of Christ,
> the newly professed religious come to the altar to receive communion
> which may be given to them under both kinds. Then their parents,
> relatives, and fellow religious may receive communion in the same
> way.*

CONCLUDING RITE

SOLEMN BLESSING

> 76.   *When the prayer after communion has been said, the newly
> consecrated religious stand before the altar, and the celebrant, facing
> them, may say:*

God inspires all holy desires and brings them to fulfillment.
May he protect you always by his grace
so that you may fulfill the duties of your vocation
with a faithful heart.

R.   Amen.

May he make each of you a witness
and sign of his love for all people.

R.   Amen.

May he make those bonds,
with which he has bound you to Christ on earth,
endure for ever in heavenly love.

R.   Amen.

Another form of the blessing may be found in no. 144

77.   *Finally, the celebrant blesses the whole congregation:*

May almighty God,
the Father, and the Son, + and the Holy Spirit,
bless all of you who have taken part in this celebration.

R.   Amen.

CHAPTER IV
Rite for Renewal of Vows During Mass

78.   Renewal of vows, which is governed by the general law of the Church or by a particular ruling of the constitutions, may take place during Mass if the religious community thinks it appropriate.

79.   The rite for the renewal of vows should be conducted with the greatest simplicity, especially if, in accordance with the constitutions of the religious institute, vows are renewed frequently or annually.

80.   Either the Mass corresponding to the liturgy of the day or the ritual Mass for the day of the renewal of vows is used, in accordance with the rubrics (see Introduction, no. 9).

81.   In clerical institutes it is proper for the superior who receives the renewal of vows to preside over the eucharistic sacrifice. In lay

institutes a chair should be prepared in a convenient part of the sanctuary for the superior who is to receive the profession of his fellow religious.

82.   Religious who renew their profession may receive communion under both kinds. If only one chalice is used, it should be sufficiently large.

OUTLINE OF THE RITE

LITURGY OF THE WORD
RENEWAL OF VOWS
Prayer for God's Grace
Renewal of Profession
General Intercessions

LITURGY OF THE EUCHARIST

LITURGY OF THE WORD

83.   *In the liturgy of the word, all takes place as usual except for the following:*

a) the readings may be taken from the Mass of the day or from the texts set out in nos. 91–136 (see Introduction, nos. 9–10);
b) the profession of faith may be omitted, even if prescribed by the rubrics of the day.

84.   *After the gospel a homily which uses the readings from Scripture to emphasize the meaning and the value of religious life is given.*

RENEWAL OF VOWS

PRAYER FOR GOD'S GRACE

85.   *After the homily the celebrant prays for God's help, saying:*

God our Father gives us the grace to persevere in our resolutions.
Let us pray to him for these servants of his
who are resolved to renew their vows today in the presence
    of the Church.

All pray for a time in silence. Then the celebrant says:

Lord,
in your providence
you have called these servants of yours
to be perfect as the Gospel teaches.
In your mercy grant that they may persevere to the end
along the way of your love
on which they have set out with such joy.

We ask this through Christ our Lord.

R.   Amen.

RENEWAL OF PROFESSION

86.   *After the prayer, if it is the custom of the religious community, two members of the community stand near the celebrant (or superior) to act as witnesses. Those who are to renew their profession come, one by one, to the celebrant (or superior) and read the formula of profession.*

If there is a large number renewing their vows, the formula of profession may be recited by all. The concluding words, This I promise . . . *or the like, must be said by each individually, as a clear expression of his will.*

GENERAL INTERCESSIONS

87. *The rite fittingly concludes with the recitation of the general intercessions (prayer of the faithful); for these the formula set out in nos. 140–142 may be used.*

LITURGY OF THE EUCHARIST

88. *During the offertory song some of the religious who have renewed their vows may bring the bread, wine, and water to the altar for the eucharistic sacrifice.*

89. *The celebrant, after saying,* The peace of the Lord, *gives to each of the religious who have renewed their vows the sign of peace in the usual way or in accordance with the custom of the place or of the religious community. If there are many, he gives the sign of peace to the first, who gives it to the rest.*

90. *After the celebrant has received the body and blood of Christ, the religious who have renewed their vows come to the altar to receive communion under both kinds.*

CHAPTER V
Other Texts for the Rites of Religious Profession

I. BIBLICAL READINGS

READINGS FROM THE OLD TESTAMENT

91. Genesis 12:1–4a—*Leave your country, your family, and come.*

92. 1 Samuel 3:1–10—*Speak, Lord, your servant in listening.*

93. 1 Kings 19:4–9a, 11–15a—*Go out and stand on the mountain before the Lord.*

94. 1 Kings 19:16b, 19–21—*Elisha left and followed Elijah.*

READINGS FROM THE NEW TESTAMENT

95. Acts 2:42–47—*All those who believed were equal and held everything in common.*

96. Acts 4:32–35—*One heart and one soul.*

97. Romans 6:3–11—*Let us walk in newness of life.*

98. Romans 12:1–13—*Offer your bodies as a living, holy sacrifice, truly pleasing to God.*

99. 1 Corinthians 1:22–31—*To many, preaching a crucified Christ is madness; to us, it is the power of God.*

100. Ephesians 1:3–14—*The Father chose us in Christ to be holy and spotless in love.*

101. Philippians 2:1–4—*Be united in your convictions and in your love.*

102. Philippians 3:8–14—*I look on everything as useless if only I can know Christ.*

103. Colossians 3:1–4—*Let your thoughts be on heavenly things, not on the things that are on the earth.*

104. Colossians 3:12–17—*Above everything, have love for each other because that is the bond of perfection.*

105. 1 Thessalonians 4:1–3a, 7–12—*What God wants is for you to be holy.*

106. 1 Peter 1:3–9—*You have not seen the Christ, yet you love him.*

107. 1 John 4:7–16—*As long as we love one another God will live in us.*

108. Revelation 3:14b, 20–22—*I shall share a meal side by side with him.*

109. Revelation 22:12–14, 16–17, 20—*Come Lord Jesus!*

RESPONSORIAL PSALMS

110. Psalm 24:1–2, 3–4ab, 5–6

　　R. (v.6):　Lord, this is the people that longs to see your face.

111. Psalm 27:1, 4, 5, 8b–9abc, 9d and 11

　　R. (v.8b):　I long to see your face, O Lord.

112. Psalm 33:2–3, 4–5, 11–12, 13–14, 18–19, 20–21

　　R. (v.12b):　Happy the people the Lord has chosen to be his own.

113. Psalm 34:2–3, 4–5, 6–7, 8–9 or 10–11, 12–13, 14–15, 17, and 19

　　R. (v.2a):　I will bless the Lord at all times.
　　or (v.9a):　Taste and see the goodness of the Lord.

114. Psalm 40:2 and 4ab, 7–8a, 8b–9 10, 12

　　R. (v.8a and 9a):　Here am I, Lord; I come to do your will.

115. Psalm 63:2, 3–4, 5–6, 8–9

　　R. (v.2b):　My soul is thirsting for you, O Lord my God.

116. Psalm 84:3, 4, 5–6a and 8a, 11, 12

　　R. (v.2):　How lovely is your dwelling place, Lord, mighty God!

117. Psalm 100:2, 3, 4, 5

　　R. (v.2c):　Come with joy into the presence of the Lord.

ALLELUIA VERSE AND VERSE BEFORE THE GOSPEL

118. Psalm 133:1
　　See how good it is, how pleasant,
　　that brothers and sisters live in unity.

119. Matthew 11:25
　　Blessed are you, Father, Lord of heaven and earth;
　　you have revealed to little ones the mysteries of the kingdom.

120. John 13:34
　　I give you a new commandment:
　　love one another as I have loved you.

121. John 15:5
    I am the vine and you are the branches, says the Lord:
    those who live in me, and I in them, will bear much fruit.

122. 2 Corinthians 8:9
    Jesus Christ was rich but he became poor
    to make you rich out of his poverty.

123. Galatians 6:14
    My only glory is the cross of our Lord Jesus Christ,
    which crucifies the world to me and me to the world.

124. Philippians 3:8–9
    I count all things worthless but this:
    to gain Jesus Christ and to be found in him.

GOSPEL

125. Matthew 11:25–30—*You have hidden these things from the learned and clever and revealed them to little children.*

126. Matthew 16:24–27—*Any who lose their life for my sake will find it.*

127. Matthew 19:3–12—*There are some persons who choose to remain unmarried for the sake of the kingdom of heaven.*

128. Matthew 19:16–26—*If you wish to be perfect, go and sell everything you have and come, follow me.*

129. Mark 3:31–35—*Who ever does the will of God is my brother, my sister, and my mother.*

130. Mark 10:24b–30—*We have left everything and have followed you.*

131. Luke 9:57–62—*Once the hand is laid on the plough, no one who looks back is fit for the kingdom of God.*

132. Luke 11:27–28—*Happy are they who hear the word of God and keep it.*

133. John 12:24–26—*If a grain of wheat falls on the ground and dies, it yields a rich harvest.*

134. John 15:1–8—*Those who live in me, and I in them, will bear much fruit.*

135. John 15:9–17—*You are friends if you do what I command you.*

136. John 17:20–26—*I want those you have given me to be with me where I am.*

II. ANOTHER FORM FOR PRESENTING THE INSIGNIA OF FIRST PROFESSION

PRESENTATION OF THE HABIT

137. After the profession the celebrant (or superior) assisted by the novice master gives the religious habit to each of the professed with these or similar words:

Receive this habit as a sign of your consecration.
May you be as closely united to the Lord in your heart
as it proclaims you to be.

The professed replies:

R.   Amen.

They put on the habit in some convenient place. After one or two have received the habit the choir may begin the antiphon:

Lord, these are the men who long to see your face,
who seek the face of the God of Jacob (Psalm 24:6),

with Psalm 24; or some other appropriate song may be sung. The antiphon is repeated after every two verses; at the end of the psalm Glory to the Father is not said but only the antiphon. If the presentation of the insignia comes to an end before the whole psalm is sung, the psalm is interrupted and the antiphon repeated.

138. Then, if customary, the newly professed, wearing the religious habit, come to the celebrant (or superior) one by one. He gives the book of the rule or constitutions to each of them, saying these or similar words:

Receive the rule of our (this) religious community.
By keeping it faithfully, may you arrive at the perfection of love.

The professed replies:

R.   Amen.

After receiving the book, he returns to his place and remains standing.

139. *If the newly professed are numerous, or there is some other reason, the celebrant (or superior) may present each of them with the rule and habit and say the formula once for all.*

If, in accordance with the rules or customs of the religious community, other signs of religious profession are to be presented, this is done now in silence or with a suitable formula. In this matter a dignified simplicity should be observed.

III. OPTIONAL GENERAL INTERCESSIONS

INTRODUCTION

140.   *a) In the Mass of first profession:*

Dear friends (brothers),
today our community rejoices in the Lord,
because these servants of his desire by their religious profession
to be more generous
in their service of God and of his Church.
Let us in unity of heart pray to God our Father
who gives to each the grace of his vocation.

b) In the Mass of renewal of vows:

Dear friends (brothers),
let us pray to God our Father for his Church,
for the peace and salvation of the world,
for our own community,
and especially for our brothers who have renewed their vows today.

INTENTIONS

141.
I.   a) For the holy Church of God,
             that adorned by the virtues of her children
             she may shine ever more brightly for Christ,
                  her Bridegroom:
             let us pray to the Lord.

I.   b) For our holy father the Pope and the other
            bishops,
         that by sound teaching and loving care
         they may be faithful shepherds of God's holy
            people:
         let us pray to the Lord.

II.   a) For the peace and salvation of the world,
         that all religious may be messengers and
            servants of the peace of Christ:
         let us pray to the Lord.

      b) For the good of all people,
         that those who are dedicated to the
            Lord's service
         may pursue the things of heaven
         and spend their days in the service
            of others:
         let us pray to the Lord.

      c) For all who believe in Christ,
         that they may listen attentively to the secret
            voice of God
         as he invites them all to a life of holiness:
         let us pray to the Lord.

      d) For the poor and suffering,
         that Christ's example may always inspire
            religious
         to bring the good news to the poor,
         to care for the sick and to comfort the afflicted:
         let us pray to the Lord.

III. a) For all religious,
         that their way of life
         may be a sign to all of the future world to come:
         let us pray to the Lord.

      b) For those who follow the evangelical counsels,
         that the law of love may shine in their lives,
         and that like the first disciples
         they may be one in heart and mind:
         let us pray to the Lord.

c) For all religious,
   that each one, according to the call of God,
   may increase the holiness of the Church
   and work to spread God's kingdom:
   let us pray to the Lord.

IV. a) For these brothers of ours
     who have today bound themselves more closely
        to God
     by religious profession,
     that in his goodness he may give them a love
        of prayer,
     a spirit of penance,
     and zeal in the apostolate:
     let us pray to the Lord.

   b) For these brothers of ours
      who have today
      bound themselves more closely to God's service,
      that their hearts may be filled
      with generous love for all:
      let us pray to the Lord.

   c) For those who today make profession of the
         evangelical counsels,
      that religious consecration may increase the holiness
      to which baptism has called them:
      let us pray to the Lord.

   d) For those who seek to follow Christ
      more closely by religious profession,
      that their chastity may show the fruitfulness
         of the Church,
      their poverty serve those in need,
      and their obedience lead the rebellious
      to accept the gentle rule of Christ:
      let us pray to the Lord.

   e) For all Christ's faithful people,
      that the whole Church
      may be the light of the world
      and the heaven in its midst

to renew society by holy living and hidden prayer:
let us pray to the Lord.

f) For all here present,
that we may be faithful to Christ's teaching
as he calls us to be perfect,
and that we may bear fruit in holiness,
grow into the fullness of Christ,
and meet together in the heavenly city of peace:
let us pray to the Lord.

CONCLUDING PRAYER

142.   *a) In the Mass of the first profession:*

Lord,
hear the prayers of your people.
In your goodness you called these servants of yours
to follow Christ and to be perfect.
Through the intercession of the Blessed Virgin Mary,
the mother of the Church,
pour forth your Holy Spirit upon them
so that they may fulfill in their whole lives
the promise they have made today.

We ask this through Christ our Lord.

R.   Amen.

b) In the Mass of renewal of vows:

Lord God,
all holiness is from you.
In your goodness hear the prayers of your family,
and by the intercession of Blessed Mary, your handmaid,
pour forth your blessings in abundance upon these servants of yours,
so that by your continued help
they may fulfill the vows
your love has inspired them to renew.

We ask this through Christ our Lord.

R.   Amen.

IV. ANOTHER SOLEMN PRAYER OF BLESSING OR CONSECRATION OF THE PROFESSED

143.
Lord God,
source of holiness and growth in your Church,
all creation owes you its debt of praise.
In the beginning of time
you created the world to share your joy.
When it lay broken by Adam's sin,
you promised a new heaven and a new earth.
You entrusted the earth to the care of men and women
to be made fruitful by their work.
Living in this world they were to direct their steps
to the heavenly city.
By your sacraments
you make us your children
and welcome us into your Church;
you distribute among us
the many gifts of your Spirit.
Some serve you in chaste marriage;
others forego marriage for the sake of your kingdom.
Sharing all things in common,
with one heart and mind in the bond of love,
they become a sign of the communion of heaven.

Father, we pray now,
send your Spirit upon these servants of yours
who have committed themselves
with steadfast faith
to the words of Christ your Son.
Strengthen their understanding
and direct their lives by the teaching of the Gospel.
May the law of love rule in their hearts,
and concern for others distinguish their lives,
so that they may bear witness to you, the one true God,
and to your infinite love for all people
By their courage in daily trials
may they receive, even in this life,

your promised hundredfold,
and at the end an everlasting reward in heaven.

. We ask this through Christ our Lord.

R.   Amen.

V. ANOTHER FORM OF BLESSING AT THE END OF THE MASS OF PERPETUAL PROFESSION

144.
May God, who is the source of all good intentions,
enlighten your minds and strengthen your hearts.
May he help you to fulfill with steadfast faith
     all you have promised.

R.   Amen.

May the Lord enable you to travel in the joy of Christ
as you follow along his way,
and may you gladly share each other's burdens.

R.   Amen.

May the love of God unite you and make you a true family
praising his name and showing forth Christ's love.

R.   Amen.

May almighty God,
the Father, and the Son, + and the Holy Spirit,
bless all of you who have taken part in these sacred celebrations

R.   Amen.

PART II
Rite of Religious Profession for Women

CHAPTER I
Norms for the Rite of Initiation into the Religious Life

1.   On the day when the canonical novitiate begins, it is fitting that there should be a ceremony to ask God's grace for achieving the special purpose of the novitiate.

2.   It is forbidden to perform the rite of initiation during Mass.

3.   The rite is to be very simple and direct, in the presence of the religious community only.

4.   The texts for the rite must avoid anything that may seem to diminish the novices' freedom of choice or obscure the true meaning of a noviceship or time of testing.

5.   The chapter hall or other similar room is an appropriate setting for the rite. If it seems necessary, however, the rite may take place in the chapel.

OUTLINE OF THE RITE

INTRODUCTORY RITES

Greeting or Song
Questioning of the Postulants or Request for Admission
Prayer

CELEBRATION OF THE WORD OF GOD

CONCLUDING RITES

General Intercessions
Lord's Prayer
Concluding Prayer

It is appropriate that the rite should take place during a special celebration of the word on the nature of the religious life and the spirit of the institute.

INTRODUCTORY RITES

GREETING OR SONG

6.   *The rite may appropriately begin with a greeting by the superior, or the singing of a psalm or other suitable hymn.*

QUESTIONING OF THE POSTULANTS OR REQUEST FOR ADMISSION

7.   *Then the superior questions the postulants in these or similar words:*

Dear daughters (sisters), what do you ask from us?

The postulants reply together in these or similar words:

We wish to try your way of life,
and are willing to be tested ourselves,
that we may follow Christ wholeheartedly
in this community of N.

The superior replies:

May the Lord grant you his help.

R.   Amen.

8.   *The questioning may be omitted, and the request for admission takes place as follows: one of the postulants, facing the superior and community, speaks in the name of all:*

Drawn by God's mercy,
we have come here to learn your way of life.
We ask you to teach us to follow Christ crucified
and to live in poverty, obedience and chastity.
Teach us to persevere in prayer and penance,
in the service of the Church and of humankind.
Teach us to be one with you in heart and mind.
Help us to live out the Gospel every day of our lives.

Teach us your rule and help us to learn to love
our sisters as Christ commanded us.

> *Or she may use similar words, expressing the aspirations and thoughts of the postulants themselves.*

> *The superior responds in these or similar words:*

May God in his mercy be with you always,
and may Christ our teacher grant light to us all.

R.   Amen.

9.   *After the questioning or request for admission, the superior says:*

Let us pray.

Lord God,
you give us the desire to hear your call.
Listen favorably to the prayers of your servants N. and N.,
who, desiring to serve you more perfectly,
ask to join our community.
Grant that our life in common
may become a communion of love.

We ask this through Christ our Lord.

R.   Amen.

CELEBRATION OF THE WORD OF GOD

10.   *Suitable texts from holy Scripture are then read, with appropriate responsories (see nos. 98–152).*

11.   *At their conclusion the superior addresses the religious community and the postulants on the meaning of the religious life and the spirit of the institute, or she reads an appropriate chapter of the rule.*

CONCLUDING RITES

12.   *The rite fittingly concludes with the general intercessions (prayer of the faithful) and the Lord's Prayer, to which a suitable prayer may be added, such as:*

God our Father,
it is you who have called us.
Hear our prayers and bless these sisters of ours
who wish to follow your Son in religious life.
Help us all to do what you ask of us
so that your plans for them may be fulfilled.

We ask this through Christ our Lord.

R.   Amen.

> 13.   *After this the superior entrusts the newly admitted novices to the care of the novice mistress, and with her fellow religious greets them in the spirit of Christian love in the way customary in the religious community. Meanwhile, an appropriate song or a canticle of praise is sung.*

CHAPTER II
Rite of Temporary Profession During Mass

14.   The rite described in this chapter takes place during Mass. It may be used only for those religious who make their first profession upon successful completion of the novitiate (see Introduction, no. 5).

Blessing of the Habit on the Day Before Profession

> 15.   *It is appropriate to give the religious habit, with the exception of the veil, to the novices the day before their first profession.*

> 16.   *The habits, but not the veils, are blessed by a priest or other competent minister, using this or a similar prayer:*

V.   Our help is in the name of the Lord.
R.   Who made heaven and earth.

V.   The Lord be with you.
R.   And also with you.

Let us pray.

God, you clothed your Son with our mortal flesh
in the chaste womb of the Virgin Mary;
give a rich blessing to these habits,
and grant that your servants who wear them on earth
may be a sign of the resurrection to come
and be clothed in the glory of eternal life.

We ask this through Christ our Lord.

R.   Amen.

The habits may then be sprinkled with holy water.

17.   At an appointed time, the superior assembles the community and the novices; in a brief address she prepares the minds of all for the rite of profession to take place the following day. Then she gives the religious habit, with the exception of the veil, to each novice so that she may wear it for the entrance procession at the beginning of Mass.

18.   The Mass may correspond to the liturgy of the day, or the ritual Mass for the day of first profession may be used, in accordance with the rubrics (see Introduction no. 9–11).

19.   The profession ordinarily takes place at the chair. A chair for the superior who is to receive the sisters' profession should be prepared in a suitable place in the sanctuary. Seats should be so arranged in the sanctuary for those making profession that the faithful have a complete view of the liturgical rites.

20.   Religious bound by the law of enclosure may make their temporary profession in the sanctuary, with due respect for the general laws of the Church and the particular occasion.

21.   Enough bread and wine for consecration should be prepared for the ministers, those making their profession, and their parents, relatives, and fellow religious. If only one chalice is used, it should be sufficiently large.

22.   In addition to what is needed for Mass, there should also be ready:

a) The ritual for religious profession;

b) the religious veils, if the religious institute has decided to present them on the occasion of first profession (see Introduction, no. 5);

c) the book of the rule or constitutions, and other insignia of religious profession which, according to law or custom, are to be presented.

OUTLINE OF THE RITE

INTRODUCTORY RITES

LITURGY OF THE WORD

RELIGIOUS PROFESSION
Calling or Request
Homily or Address
Examination
Prayer for God's Grace
Profession
Presentation of the Insignia of Religious Profession
  Presentation of the Veil
  Presentation of the Rule or Constitutions
General Intercessions

LITURGY OF THE EUCHARIST

INTRODUCTORY RITES

23.   *When the people and the religious are assemble and everything is ready, the procession moves through the church to the altar in the usual way, while the choir and people sing the entrance song of the Mass. Those to be professed may fittingly join in this procession, accompanied by the superior and the novice mistress.*

24.   *When they come to the sanctuary all make the customary reverence to the altar and go to their places; then Mass continues.*

LITURGY OF THE WORD

25.   *The liturgy of the word takes place as usual, except for the following:*
    a) the readings may be taken from the Mass of the day or from the texts in nos. 98–152 (see Introduction, nos. 9–10);
    b) the profession of faith may be omitted, even if prescribed the rubrics of the day.

RELIGIOUS PROFESSION

CALLING OR REQUEST

26.   *After the gospel the celebrant and the people sit, but those to be professed stand. Then, according to choice or as circumstances demand, the deacon or the novice mistress calls those to be professed by name.*

They answer:

Lord, you have called me; here I am,

    or they make some other reply according to local usage or the custom of the religious community.

27.   *The celebrant then questions them in these or similar words:*

My dear sisters (daughters), what do you ask of God and of his holy Church?

The candidates reply together in these or similar words:

We ask for God's merciful love
and a share in this religious community of N.

The celebrant and all the members of the religious community reply:

Thanks be to God,

or they express their approval in some other way.

28. *The calling by name and the questioning by the celebrant may be omitted; a request by those to be professed may take their place. For example, one of those to be professed may stand facing the superior and say, in the name of all, these or similar words:*

With the help of God,
we (N. and N.) have studied your rule
and have lived among you as your sisters for the time of probation.
Mother (Sister), we now ask to be allowed
to dedicate ourselves to God and his kingdom
by making profession in this religious community of N.

The superior and all the members of the religious community reply:

Thanks be to God,

or they express their approval in some other way.

Homily or Address

29. *Those to be professed then sit and listen to the homily or address which should develop the scriptural readings and the theme of religious profession as God's gift and call for the sanctification of those chosen and for the good of the Church and the whole human family.*

Examination

30. *After the homily or address, those to be professed stand, and the celebrant questions them on their readiness to dedicate themselves to God and to seek perfect charity, according to the rule or constitutions of the religious community. The questions may be changed or in part omitted, to suit the spirit and character of each religious institute.*

My dear sisters (daughters),
by water and the Holy Spirit
you have already been consecrated to God's service:
are you resolved to unite yourselves more closely to him
by the new bond of religious profession?

They answer:

I am.

The celebrant continues:

In your desire to follow Christ perfectly,
are you resolved to live in chastity
for the sake of the kingdom of heaven,
to choose a life of poverty,
and to offer the sacrifice of obedience?

They answer:

I am.

31.   *Then the celebrant confirms their intention in these or similar words:*

May almighty God grant you his grace
to fulfill what you resolve.

R.   Amen.

PRAYER FOR GOD'S GRACE

32.   *The celebrant then prays for God's help, saying:*

Let us pray.

All pray for a while in silence. Then the celebrant says:

Lord,
look upon these servants of yours
who are resolved to dedicate their lives to you
by making profession of the evangelical counsels
in the presence of your Church today.
Mercifully grant that their manner of life
may bring glory to your name
and further your loving plan of redemption.

We ask this through Christ our Lord.

R.   Amen.

PROFESSION

33.   *After the prayer, if it is the custom of the religious community, two professed religious stand near the superior to act as witnesses. Those to be professed come, one by one, to the celebrant and read the formula of profession.*

If there are very many religious making their profession, the formula of profession may be recited by all together. The concluding words, This I promise . . . *or the like, must be said by each individually, as a clear expression of her will.*

After the profession, they return to their places and remain standing.

PRESENTATION OF THE INSIGNIA OF RELIGIOUS PROFESSION

PRESENTATION OF THE VEIL

34.   After this, if the veil is to be presented, the celebrant, with the assistance of the superior and the mistress of novices, clothes each one with the veil, saying, for example:

Receive this veil
which proclaims
that you belong entirely to Christ the Lord
and are dedicated to the service of the Church.

R.   Amen.

PRESENTATION OF THE RULE OR CONSTITUTIONS

35.   Then, where it is the custom, the celebrant gives her the book of the rule or constitutions, using this or a similar formula:

Receive the rule of this religious community,
and show in your whole life
what you have faithfully learned.

The professed replies:

R.   Amen.

After receiving the book, she returns to her place.

36.   After the first or second of the professed has received the veil and rule, the choir intones the antiphon:

I have sought the Lord whom I love with all my heart
(Song of Song 3:4),

with Psalm 45; or some other appropriate song may be sung. The antiphon is repeated after every two verses; at the end of the psalm Glory to the Father *is not said but only the antiphon. If the presentation of the insignia comes to an end before the whole psalm is sung, the psalm is interrupted and the antiphon repeated.*

37.   *If, in accordance with the rules or customs of the religious community, other insignia of religious profession are to be presented, this is done now in silence or with a suitable formula. In this matter a dignified simplicity should be observed.*

38.   *An alternative way of presenting the insignia of profession is described in nos. 153–155.*

GENERAL INTERCESSIONS

39.   *The rite fittingly concludes with the general intercessions (prayer of the faithful). For these, the formula given in nos. 156–158 may be used.*

LITURGY OF THE EUCHARIST

40.   *During the offertory song, some of the newly professed religious may bring the bread, wine, and water to the altar for the eucharistic sacrifice.*

41.   *The celebrant gives the sign of peace in some suitable way to the newly professed religious and all those present.*

42.   *After the celebrant has received the body and blood of Christ, the newly professed religious come to the altar to receive communion which may be given to them under both kinds. Then their parents, relatives, and fellow religious may receive communion in the same way.*

CHAPTER III
Rite of Perpetual Profession During Mass

43.   It is fitting that the rite of profession by which a religious binds herself to God for ever should take place on a Sunday or a solemnity of the Lord, of the Blessed Virgin Mary, or of a saint distinguished in the living of the religious life.

44.   The rite of perpetual profession takes place separately from other rites of profession (see Introduction, no. 8).

45.   Notice of the day and hour should be given to the faithful in good time so that they may attend in greater numbers.

46.   The Mass is that of the liturgy of the day, or the ritual Mass for the day of perpetual religious profession may be used, in accordance with the rubrics (see Introduction, nos. 9–11).

47.   Where possible and if the needs of the faithful do not demand individual celebrations by the priests present, it is preferable that the Mass be concelebrated.

48.   The profession ordinarily takes place at the chair. A chair for the superior who is to receive the profession of the sisters should be prepared in a suitable place in the sanctuary. Seats should be so arranged in the sanctuary for those making profession that the faithful may have a complete view of the liturgical rites.

49.   It is fitting that religious bound by the law of enclosure also make their perpetual profession in the sanctuary.

50.   Profession ordinarily takes place in the church of the religious community. For pastoral reasons, however, or in order to promote esteem for the religious life, to give edification to the people of God, or to permit larger attendance, the rite may take place in the cathedral, parish church, or some other notable church, as may seem fitting.

51.   Similarly, where religious from two or more institutes wish to celebrate their profession at the same eucharistic sacrifice, the rite of profession may suitably take place in the cathedral, parish church, or other notable church with the bishop presiding. Those making their profession will pronounce their vows before their respective superiors.
    Enclosed religious, however, are to observe carefully the laws of their enclosure in this matter.

52.   As the nature of the rite demands, the whole liturgical service should be celebrated with fitting solemnity, but any appearance of lavishness unbecoming to religious poverty should be avoided.

53.   Enough bread and wine for consecration should be prepared for the ministers, those making their profession, and their parents, relatives, and fellow religious. If only one chalice is used, it should be sufficiently large.

54. In addition to what is needed for Mass, there should also be ready:

a) the ritual for religious profession;
b) the rings and other insignia of religious profession, if these are to be presented in accordance with the rules or customs of the religious community.

OUTLINE OF THE RITE

INTRODUCTORY RITES

LITURGY OF THE WORD

RELIGIOUS PROFESSION
Calling or Request
Homily or Address
Examination
Litany
Profession
Solemn Blessing or Consecration of the Professed
Presentation of the Insignia of Profession
Statement of Admission or Sign of Peace

LITURGY OF THE EUCHARIST

CONCLUDING RITE
Solemn Blessing

INTRODUCTORY RITES

55.   When the people and the religious are assembled and everything is ready, the procession moves through the church to the altar in the usual way, while the choir and people sing the entrance song of the Mass. Those to be professed may join in the procession, accompanied by the superior and the novice mistress.

56.   When they come to the sanctuary, all make the customary reverence to the altar and go to their places; then Mass continues.

LITURGY OF THE WORD

57.   The liturgy of the word takes place as usual, except for the following:

   a) the readings may be taken from the Mass of the day or from the texts in nos. 98–152 (see Introduction, nos. 9–10);
   b) the profession of faith may be omitted, even if prescribed by the rubrics of the day.
   c) the general intercessions in the form customarily used during the celebration of Mass are omitted (see no. 67).

RELIGIOUS PROFESSION

CALLING OR REQUEST

58.   After the gospel the celebrant and the people sit, but those to be professed stand. Then, according to choice or as circumstances demand, the deacon or the novice mistress calls those to professed by name.

They answer:

Lord, you have called me; here I am,

   or they make some other reply according to local usage or the custom of the religious community.

59.   The celebrant then questions them in these or similar words:

My dear sisters (daughters), what do you ask of God and of his holy Church?

The candidates reply together in these or similar words:

175

We ask for perseverance
in following Christ our Bridegroom
in this religious community
all the days of our lives.

> *The celebrant, superior, and all the members of the religious community reply:*

Thanks be to God,

> *or they express their approval in some other way.*

---

60. *The calling by name and the questioning by the celebrant may be omitted; a request by those to be professed may take their place. For example, one of those to be professed may stand facing the superior and say, in the name of all, these or similar words:*

With the help of God,
we (N. and N.) have come to know in your religious community
the difficulty and the joy of a life completely dedicated to him.
Mother (Sister), we now ask to be allowed
to make perpetual profession in this community of N.
for the glory of God and the service of the Church.

> *The superior and all the members of the religious community reply:*

Thanks be to God,

> *or they express their approval in some other way.*

HOMILY OR ADDRESS

> 61. *Those to be professed then sit and listen to the homily or address which should develop the scriptural readings and the theme of religious profession as God's gift and call for the sanctification of those chosen and for the good of the Church and the whole human family.*

EXAMINATION

> 62. *After the homily or address, those to be professed stand, and the celebrant questions them on their readiness to dedicate themselves to God and to seek perfect charity, according to the rule or constitutions of the religious community. The questions may be changed or in part omitted, to suit the spirit and character of each religious institute.*

Dear sisters (daughters),
in baptism you have already died to sin

and have been set aside for God's service.
Are you now resolved to unite yourself more closely to God
by the bond of perpetual profession?

They answer:

I am.

The celebrant continues:

Are you resolved,
with the help of God,
to undertake that life of perfect chastity, obedience, and poverty
chosen for themselves by Christ our Lord and his Virgin Mother,
and to persevere in it for ever?

They answer:

I am.

The celebrant continues:

Are you resolved to strive steadfastly for perfection
in the love of God and of your neighbor
by living the Gospel with all your heart
and keeping the rule of this religious community?

They answer:

I am.

The celebrant continues:

Are you resolved,
with the help of the Holy Spirit,
to spend your whole life in the generous service of God's people?

They answer:

I am.

63.   *In the case of religious communities wholly dedicated to the
contemplative life, this may appropriately be added:
The celebrant asks:*

Are you resolved to live for God alone,
in solitude and silence,
in persevering prayer and willing penance,
in humble work and holiness of life?

They answer:

I am.

64. At the end of the questions, the celebrant confirms the intention of those to be professed in these or similar words:

May God who has begun the good work in you
bring it to fulfillment
before the day of Christ Jesus.

All:

Amen.

LITANY

65. All then rise. The celebrant stands, with hands joined, and says, facing the people:

Dear friends in Christ,
let us pray to God the almighty Father
who gives us everything that is good:
in his mercy may he strengthen his servants
in the purpose he has inspired in them.

61. The deacon gives the sign to kneel.

Let us kneel.

The celebrant at his chair, the ministers, those to be professed and the people kneel. Where there is the custom of prostration of those to be professed, this may be kept. During the Easter Season and on all Sundays, all stand except those to be professed.

67. Then the cantors sing the litany for the rite of religious profession, all making the responses. In this litany one or other of the petitions marked with the same letter may be omitted. At the appropriate place there may be inserted invocations of saints especially venerated in the religious community or by the faithful; other petitions may be added to suit the occasion.

Lord, have mercy	Lord, have mercy
Christ, have mercy	Christ, have mercy
Lord, have mercy	Lord, have mercy
Holy Mary, Mother of God	pray for us
Saint Michael	pray for us

Holy angels of God	pray for us
Saint John the Baptist	pray for us
Saint Joseph	pray for us
Saint Peter and Saint Paul	pray for us
Saint John	pray for us
Saint Mary Magdalene	pray for us
Saint Stephen and Saint Lawrence	pray for us
Saint Agnes	pray for us
Saint Basil	pray for us
Saint Augustine	pray for us
Saint Benedict	pray for us
Saint Francis and Saint Dominic	pray for us
Saint Macrina	pray for us
Saint Scholastica	pray for us
Saint Clare and Saint Catherine	pray for us
Saint Teresa of Jesus	pray for us
Saint Rose of Lima	pray for us
Saint Jane Frances de Chantal	pray for us
Saint Louise de Marillac	pray for us
All holy men and women	pray for us
Lord, be merciful	Lord, save your people
From all evil	Lord, save your people
From every sin	Lord, save your people
From everlasting death	Lord, save your people
By your coming as man	Lord, save your people
By your death and rising to new life	Lord, save your people
By your gift of the Holy Spirit	Lord, save your people
Be merciful to us sinners	Lord, hear our prayer

a) By the self-offering of your servants
and their apostolic work,
make the life of your Church
ever more fruitful.   Lord, hear our prayer

a) Give in ever greater abundance
the gifts of the Holy Spirit
to your servant, Pope N.,
and to all his brother bishops.   Lord, hear our prayer

b) By the life and labor of all religious promote the welfare of all people.	Lord, hear our prayer
b) Lead all men and women to the fullness of the Christian life.	Lord, hear our prayer
c) Grant that all religious families may live and grow in the love of Christ and the spirit of their founders.	Lord, hear our prayer
c) Give to all who profess the Gospel counsels a fuller share in the work of redemption.	Lord, hear our prayer
d) Reward a hundredfold the parents of your servants for the sacrifice they have made.	Lord, hear our prayer
e) Make these servants of yours more and more like Christ, the firstborn among many.	Lord, hear our prayer
e) Give these servants of yours the grace of perseverance.	Lord, hear our prayer
e) Bless these sisters of ours, your servants, make them holy, and consecrate them to your service.	Lord, hear our prayer
Jesus, Son of the living God Christ, hear us Lord Jesus, hear our prayer	Lord, hear our prayer Christ, hear us Lord Jesus, hear our prayer

68.   *Then the celebrant alone rises and says, with hands joined:*

Lord,
grant the prayers of your people.
Prepare the hearts of your servants
for consecration to your service.
By the grace of the Holy Spirit,
purify them from all sin
and set them on fire with your love.

We ask this through Christ our Lord.

R.   Amen.

> *The deacon then says:*

Let us rise.

> *All stand.*

PROFESSION

> 69.   *After the litany, if it is the custom of the religious community, two professed members of the community come to the chair of the superior and, standing, act as witnesses. Those to be professed come, one by one, to the superior and read the formula of profession, which they themselves have written out beforehand.*

> 70.   *Then the newly professed may fittingly go to the altar, one by one, to place on it the formula of profession; if it can be done conveniently, each of them should sign the document of profession upon the altar itself. After this, each goes back to her place.*

> 71.   *Afterward, if this is the practice of the community, the newly professed may stand and sing an antiphon or other song expressing the spirit of self-giving and joy, for example:*

Uphold me, Lord, according to your promise
and I shall live;
and do not bring to nothing all my hope (Psalm 119:116).

SOLEMN BLESSING OR CONSECRATION OF THE PROFESSED

> 72.   *Then the newly professed kneel; the celebrant, with hands extended over them, says the prayer of blessing* Father in heaven, our desire to serve you, *in which the words in parentheses may, to suit the occasion, be omitted, or else the prayer* Lord God, creator of the world and Father of humankind, *which is found in no. 159.*

Father in heaven,
our desire to serve you is itself your gift
and our perseverance needs your guiding hand.
How right it is that we should sing your praise.

With boundless love
you created the human family
through your Word, in the Holy Spirit,
and lifted it up into communion with yourself;

you make the human family your bride
radiant with your own likeness,
adorned with the gifts of everlasting life.

When your bride, deceived by the evil one,
broke faith with you,
you did not abandon her.
With everlasting love you renewed with your servant Noah
the covenant you had made with Adam.
[Then you chose Abraham, the man of faith,
to be the father of a people
more numerous than the stars of heaven.
By the hand of Moses
you sealed a covenant with them in the tables of the law.
Throughout the ages
there arose from this favored people
holy women renowned for devotion and courage,
justice and faith.]

In the fullness of time
you raised up the Holy Virgin from the stock of Jesse.
The Holy Spirit was to come upon her,
and your power was to overshadow her,
making her the immaculate Mother of the world's Redeemer.

He became poor, humble, and obedient,
the source and pattern of all holiness.
He formed the Church into his bride,
loving it with love so great
that he gave himself up for it
and sanctified it in his blood.

Father, in your loving wisdom
you have singled out many of your daughters
to be disciples espoused to Christ
and to receive the honor of his love.
[Holy Church shines with their rich variety,
a bride adorned with jewels,
a queen robed in grace,
a mother rejoicing in her children.]

Father, we earnestly pray you:
send the fire of the Holy Spirit

into the hearts of your daughters
to keep alive within them
the holy desire he has given them.

Lord, may the glory of baptism and holiness of life
shine in their hearts.
Strengthened by the vows of their consecration,
may they be always one with you
in loving fidelity to Christ, their only Bridegroom.
May they cherish the Church as their mother
and love the whole world as God's creation,
teaching all people to look forward in joy and hope
to the good things of heaven.

Lord, holy Father,
guide the steps of your servants
and guard them on their pilgrimage through life.
When they come at last to the throne of Christ the King,
may they not fear him as their judge,
but hear the voice of their Bridegroom
lovingly inviting them to the wedding feast of heaven.

We ask this through Christ our Lord.

R.   Amen.

PRESENTATION OF THE INSIGNIA OF PROFESSION

73.   *After the blessing of the professed, the celebrant and the people
sit; if rings are to be presented, the newly professed rise and come to the
celebrant, who gives the ring to each, saying, for example:*

Receive this ring,
for you are betrothed to the eternal King;
keep faith with your Bridegroom
so that you may come to the wedding feast of eternal joy.

The professed replies:

Amen.

Then she returns to her place.

74.   *If there are several newly professed, or if there is any other good
reason, the celebrant may use one formula for presenting the rings to
all:*

Receive this ring,
for you are betrothed to the eternal King;
keep faith with your Bridegroom
so that you may come to the wedding feast of eternal joy.

> *They reply:*

Amen.

> *They then go to the celebrant to receive the rings.*

> 75. *Meanwhile the choir and people together sing this or some other suitable antiphon:*

I am betrothed to the Son of the eternal Father,
to him who was born of the Virgin Mother
to be the Savior of all the world,

> with *Psalm 45; or some other appropriate song may be sung. The antiphon is repeated after every two verses; at the end of the psalm* Glory to the Father *is not said but only the antiphon. If the presentation of the insignia comes to an end before the whole psalm is sung, the psalm is interrupted and the antiphon repeated.*

> 76. *If, in accordance with the laws or customs of the religious community, other insignia of religious profession are to be presented, this is done now, in silence or with a suitable formula. In this matter a dignified simplicity should be observed.*

STATEMENT OF ADMISSION OR SIGN OF PEACE

> 77. *After this, if it is customary or seems opportune, there may be a ceremony to mark the fact that the newly professed religious have been admitted as lifelong members of the religious family. This can take the form of a suitable statement by the superior or of the sign of peace. For example:*

> *a) The superior says these or similar words:*

We confirm that you are now one with us
as members of this religious community of N.,
sharing all things in common with us
now and in the future.

> *She may add:*

Be faithful to the ministry the Church entrusts to you
to be carried out in its name.

The members of the community manifest their assent, saying:

R.   Amen.

b) The above may be omitted and the celebrant may give the sign of peace. The superior and the members of the community express fraternal love for the newly professed by the sign of peace or in another way, according to the custom of the religious community. Meanwhile the choir and the people sing the antiphon:

How lovely is your dwelling place, Lord, mighty God!
My soul is longing and fainting for the courts of the Lord
(Psalm 84:2–3),

with Psalm 84; or some other appropriate song may be sung.

78.   *The newly professed religious return after this to their places. The Mass continues.*

LITURGY OF THE EUCHARIST

79.   *During the offertory song, some of the newly professed may bring to the altar the bread, wine, and water for the eucharistic sacrifice.*

80.   *In the eucharistic prayers, the offering of the professed may be mentioned according to the texts below:*

a) In Eucharistic Prayer I, the special form of Father, accept this offering *is said:*

Father, accept and sanctify this offering
from your whole family and from these your servants
which we make to you on the day of their consecration.
By your grace
they join themselves more closely to your Son today.
When he comes in glory at the end of time,
may they joyfully meet him.

[Through Christ our Lord. Amen.]

b) In the intercessions of Eucharistic Prayer II, after the words and all the clergy, *there is added:*

Remember all these sisters of ours
who have left all things for your sake,
so that they may find you in all things
and by forgetting self serve the needs of all.

c) In the intercessions of Eucharistic Prayer III, after the words your Son has gained for you, *there is added:*

Lord, strengthen these servants of yours in their holy purpose,
as they strive to follow Christ your Son in consecrated holiness
by giving witness to his love in their religious life.

d) In the intercessions of Eucharistic Prayer IV, the professed may be mentioned in this way:

. . . bishop, and bishops and clergy everywhere.
Remember these our sisters who have consecrated themselves to
    you today
by the bond of religious profession.
Remember those who take part in this offering . . .

81.   *The celebrant gives the sign of peace in some suitable form to the newly professed religious and to all those present.*

82.   *After the celebrant has received the body and blood of Christ, the newly professed religious come to the altar to receive communion which may be given to them under both kinds. Then their parents, relatives, and fellow religious may receive communion in the same way.*

CONCLUDING RITE

SOLEMN BLESSING

83.   *When the prayer after communion has been said, the newly consecrated religious stand before the altar, and the celebrant, facing them, may say:*

God inspires all holy desires and brings them to fulfillment.
May he protect you always by his grace
so that you may fulfill the duties of your vocation
with a faithful heart.

R.   Amen.

May he make each of you a witness
and sign of his love for all people.

R.   Amen.

May he make those bonds,
with which he has bound you to Christ on earth,
endure for ever in heavenly love.

R.   Amen.

Another form of the blessing may be found in no. 160.

> 84.   *Finally, the celebrant blesses the whole congregation:*

May almighty God,
the Father, and the Son, + and the Holy Spirit,
bless all of you who have taken part in this celebration.

R.   Amen.

CHAPTER IV
Rite for Renewal of Vows During Mass

85.   Renewal of vows, which is governed by the general law of the church or by a particular ruling of the constitutions, may take place during Mass if the religious community thinks it appropriate.

86.   The rite for the renewal of vows should be conducted with the greatest simplicity, especially if, in accordance with the constitutions of the religious institute, vows are renewed frequently or annually.

87.   Either the Mass corresponding to the liturgy of the day or the ritual Mass for the day of the renewal of vows is used, in accordance with the rubrics (see Introduction, nos. 9–10).

88.   The renewal of vows customarily takes place before the superior, whose chair may be placed in a suitable place in the sanctuary.

89.   Religious who renew their profession may receive communion under both kinds. If only one chalice is used, it should be sufficiently large.

OUTLINE OF THE RITE

LITURGY OF THE WORD

RENEWAL OF VOWS
Prayer for God's Grace
Renewal of Profession
General Intercessions

LITURGY OF THE EUCHARIST

LITURGY OF THE WORD

90.   *In the liturgy of the word, all takes place as usual except for the following:*

a) the readings may be taken from the Mass of the day or from the texts set out in nos. 98–152 (see Introduction, nos. 9–10);
b) the profession of faith may be omitted, even if prescribed by the rubrics of the day.

91.   *After the gospel a homily which uses the readings from Scripture to emphasize the meaning and the value of the religious life is given.*

RENEWAL OF VOWS

PRAYER FOR GOD'S GRACE

92.   *After the homily the celebrant prays for God's help, saying:*

God our Father gives us the grace to persevere in our resolutions.
Let us pray to him for these servants of his
who are resolved to renew their vows today in the presence
    of the Church.

All pray for a time in silence. Then the celebrant says:

Lord,
in your providence
you have called these servants of yours
to follow your Son more closely.
Mercifully grant that they may persevere to the end
along the way of your love
on which they have set out with such joy

We ask this through Christ our Lord.

R.   Amen.

RENEWAL OF PROFESSION

93.   *After the prayer, if it is the custom of the religious community, two professed sisters stand near the superior to act as witnesses.*

Those who are to renew their profession come, one by one, to the superior and read the formula of profession. If there is a large number

renewing their vows, the formula of profession may be recited by all.
The concluding words, This I promise . . . or the like, must be said by
each individually, as a clear expression of her will.

Where profession is renewed by all each year, in accordance with the
constitutions of the institute, the superior and all the sisters should
recite the formula of profession together.

GENERAL INTERCESSIONS

94.   The rite fittingly concludes with the recitation of the general
intercessions (prayer of the faithful); for these the formula set out in
nos. 156–158 may be used.

LITURGY OF THE EUCHARIST

95.   During the offertory song some of the religious who have renewed
their vows may bring the bread, wine, and water to the altar for the
eucharistic sacrifice.

96.   The celebrant, after saying, The peace of the Lord, gives the sign
of peace in a suitable way to the religious who have just renewed their
profession and to all those present.

97.   After the celebrant has received the body and blood of Christ,
the religious who have renewed their profession come to the altar to
receive communion under both kinds.

CHAPTER V
Other Texts for the Rites of Religious Profession

I. BIBLICAL READINGS

READINGS FROM THE OLD TESTAMENT

98. Genesis 12:1–4a—*Leave your country, your family, and come.*

99. 1 Samuel 3:1–10—*Speak, Lord, your servant is listening.*

100. 1 Kings 19:4–9a, 11–15a—*Go out and stand on the mountain before the Lord.*

101. 1 Kings 19:16b, 19–21—*Elisha left and followed Elijah.*

102. Song of Songs 2:8–14—*Rise, my love, and come.*

103. Song of Songs 8:6–7—*Love is strong as death.*

104. Isaiah 61:9–11—*I exult for joy in the Lord.*

105. Hosea 2:14, 19–20 (Hebrew 16, 21–22):—*I will betroth you to myself for ever.*

READINGS FROM THE NEW TESTAMENT

106. Acts 2:42–47—*All those who believed were equal and held everything in common.*

107. Acts 4:32–35—*One heart and one soul.*

108. Romans 6:3–11—*Let us walk in newness of life.*

109. Romans 12:1–13—*Offer your bodies as a living, holy sacrifice, truly pleasing to God.*

110. 1 Corinthians 1:22–31—*To many, preaching a crucified Christ is madness; to us, it is the power of God.*

111. 1 Corinthians 7:25–35—*An unmarried woman can devote herself to the Lord's work.*

112. Ephesians 1:3–14—*The Father chose us in Christ to be holy and spotless in love.*

113. Philippians 2:1–4—*Be united in your convictions and in your love.*

114. Philippians 3:8–14—*I look on everything as useless if only I can know Christ.*

115. Colossians 3:1–4—*Let your thoughts be on heavenly things, not on the things that are on the earth.*

116. Colossians 3:12–17—*Above everything, have love for each other because that is the bond of perfection.*

117. 1 Thessalonians 4:1–3a, 7–12—*What God wants is for you to be holy.*

118. 1 Peter 1:3–9—*You have not seen the Christ, yet you love him.*

119. 1 John 4:7–16—*As long as we love one another God will live in us.*

120. Revelation 3:14b, 20–22—*I shall share a meal side by side with him.*

121. Revelation 22:12–14, 16–17, 20—*Come, Lord Jesus!*

RESPONSORIAL PSALMS

122. Psalm 24:1–2, 3–4ab, 5–6

    R. (v.6):   Lord, this is the people that longs to see your face.

123. Psalm 27:1, 4, 5, 8b–9abc, 9d, and 11

    R. (v.8b):   I long to see your face, O Lord.

124. Psalm 33:2–3, 4–5, 11–12, 13–14, 18–19, 20–21

    R. (v.12b):   Happy the people the Lord has chosen to be his own.

125. Psalm 34:2–3, 4–5, 6–7, 8–9
    or 10–11, 12–13, 14–15, 17 and 19

    R. (v.2a):   I will bless the Lord at all times.
    or (v.9a):   Taste and see the goodness of the Lord.

126. Psalm 40:2 and 4ab, 7–8a, 8b–9 10, 12

    R. (v.8a and v.9a):   Here am I, Lord; I come to do your will.

127. Psalm 45:11–12, 14–15, 16–17

    R. Matthew 25:6:   The Bridegroom is here; let us go out to meet Christ the Lord.

128. Psalm 63:2, 3–4, 5–6, 8–9

    R. (v.2b):   My soul is thirsting for you, O Lord my God.

129. Psalm 84:3, 4, 5–6a and 8a, 11, 12

    R. (v.2):   How lovely is your dwelling place, Lord, mighty God!

130. Psalm 100:2, 3, 4, 5

    R. (v.2c):   Come with joy into the presence of the Lord.

ALLELUIA VERSE AND VERSE BEFORE THE GOSPEL

131. Psalm 132:1
    See how good it is, how pleasant, that brothers and sisters live
    in unity.

132. Matthew 11:25
    Blessed are you, Father, Lord of heaven and earth:
    you have revealed to little ones the mysteries of the kingdom.

133. John 13:34
    I give you a new commandment:
    love one another as I have loved you.

134. John 15:5
    I am the vine and you are the branches, says the Lord:
    those who live in me, and I in them, will bear much fruit.

135. 2 Corinthians 8:9
    Jesus Christ was rich but he became poor
    to make you rich out of his poverty.

136. Galatians 6:14
    My only glory is the cross of our Lord Jesus Christ,
    which crucifies the world to me and me to the world.

137. Philippians 3:8–9
    I count all things worthless but this:
    to gain Jesus Christ and to be found in him.

GOSPEL

138. Matthew 11:25–30—*You have hidden these things from the
    learned and clever and revealed them to little children.*

139. Matthew 16:24–27—*Any who lose their life for my sake will
    find it.*

140. Matthew 19:3–12—*There are some persons who choose to
    remain unmarried for the sake of the kingdom of heaven.*

141. Matthew 19:16–26—*If you wish to be perfect, go and sell everything you have and come, follow me.*

142. Matthew 25:1–13—*Look, the Bridegroom is coming; go out and meet him.*

143. Mark 3:31–35—*Whoever does the will of God is my brother, my sister, and my mother.*

144. Mark 10:24b–30—*We have left everything and have followed you.*

145. Luke 1:26–38—*I am the handmaid of the Lord.*

146. Luke 9:57–62—*Once the hand is laid on the plough, no one who looks back is fit for the kingdom of God.*

147. Luke 10:38–42—*Jesus accepts the hospitality of Martha and praises the attentiveness of Mary.*

148. Luke 11:27–28—*Happy are they who hear the word of God and keep it.*

149. John 12:24–26—*If a grain of wheat falls on the ground and dies, it yields a rich harvest.*

150. John 15:1–8—*Those who live in me, and I in them, will bear much fruit.*

151. John 15:9–17—*You are friends if you do what I command you.*

152. John 17:20–26—*I want those you have given me to be with me where I am.*

II. ANOTHER FORM FOR PRESENTING THE INSIGNIA OF FIRST PROFESSION

PRESENTATION OF THE VEIL AND RITE

153. *If there are many newly professed religious, or if there is any other good reason, the celebrant presenting the insignia of profession uses this formula once for all:*

Receive, dear sisters,
this veil and rule
which are the signs of your profession.
Give yourselves wholeheartedly to Christ the Lord,
and show in your whole life
what you have faithfully learned.

The professed reply:

R.   Amen.

They come to the celebrant who, with the assistance of the superior and the mistress of novices, gives to each of them the veil and the book of the rule.

When they have received them they return to their places.

154.   Meanwhile, the choir intones the antiphon:

I have sought the Lord whom I love with all my heart (Song of Songs 3:4),

with Psalm 45; or some other appropriate song may be sung. At the end of the psalm the Glory to the Father is not said, but only the antiphon. If the presentation of the insignia comes to an end before the whole psalm is sung, the psalm is interrupted and the antiphon is repeated.

155.   If, in accordance with the rules or customs of the religious community, other insignia of religious profession are to be presented, this is done now in silence or with a suitable formula. In this matter a dignified simplicity should be observed.

III. OPTIONAL GENERAL INTERCESSIONS

INTRODUCTION

156.   a) In the Mass of first profession:

Dear friends,
as we celebrate the paschal mystery of Christ
and the first profession of these sisters,
let us pray together to God the almighty Father,
through Jesus Christ, the inspiration of religious life.

b) In the Mass of renewal of vows:

Dear friends,
Christ our Lord has told us,
"Without me you can do nothing."
Let us pray through him to the Father of all mercies
for the salvation of all people,
for peace in our time,
and for these sisters of ours who renew their vows today.

INTENTIONS

157.

I.   a) For the holy Church of God,
         that adorned by the virtues of her children
         she may shine ever more brightly for Christ,
            her Bridegroom:
         let us pray to the Lord.

       b) For our holy father the Pope and the other bishops,
         that the Holy Spirit who filled the apostles
         may pour out his grace unceasingly upon their
            successors:
         let us pray to the Lord.

       c) For all those who minister to the Church,
         that by word and work
         they may lead to salvation
         the people entrusted to their care:
         let us pray to the Lord.

II.   a) For the peace and salvation of the world,
         that all religious may be messengers and servants of
            the peace of Christ:
         let us pray to the Lord.

       b) For the good of all people,
         that those who are dedicated to the Lord's service
         may pursue the things of heaven
         and spend their days in the service of others:
         let us pray to the Lord.

       c) For all who believe in Christ,
         that they may listen attentively to the secret voice of God
         as he invites them all to a life of holiness:
         let us pray to the Lord.

III. a) For all religious,
    that they may offer
    spiritual sacrifices to God with heart and tongue,
    with hand and mind,
    in labor and suffering:
    let us pray to the Lord.

    b) For those who follow the evangelical counsels,
    that the law of love may shine in their lives,
    and that like the first disciples
    they may be one in heart and mind:
    let us pray to the Lord.

    c) For all who are consecrated to God in religion,
    that they may share the life of the Church
    and cooperate fully in all her works and hopes:
    let us pray to the Lord.

    d) For all religious,
    that each one, according to the call of God,
    may increase the holiness of the Church
    and work to spread God's kingdom:
    let us pray to the Lord.

IV. a) For these sisters of ours
    who have today bound themselves more closely to
      God
    by religious profession,
    that in his goodness he may give them a love
      of prayer,
    a spirit of penance,
    and zeal in the apostolate:
    let us pray to the Lord.

    b) For these sisters of ours
    who have today
    bound themselves more closely to God's service,
    that their hearts may be filled
    with generous love for all:
    let us pray to the Lord.

c) For these sisters of ours
   who have today dedicated themselves
      to Christ the Lord,
   that, like the wise virgins,
   they may keep alight the lamp of faith and love:
   let us pray to the Lord.

d) For these religious
   who have today sealed their desire for holiness,
   that they may keep watch for the Bridegroom,
   and so enter the wedding feast of heaven:
   let us pray to the Lord.

e) For those who today make profession of the
      evangelical counsels,
   that religious consecration may increase the holiness
   to which baptism has called them:
   let us pray to the Lord.

f) For all here present,
   that we may be faithful to Christ's teaching
   as he calls us to be perfect,
   and that we may bear fruit in holiness,
   grow into the fullness of Christ,
   and meet together in the heavenly city of peace:
   let us pray to the Lord.

CONCLUDING PRAYER

158.   *a) In the Mass of the first profession:*

Lord, protect your family,
and in your goodness grant our prayers
for these sisters of ours
as they offer you the first fruits
of their consecrated lives.

We ask this through Christ our Lord.

R.   Amen.

b) In the Mass of renewal of vows:

Lord God,
you are the source of truth and mercy.

Hear the prayers of your people,
and by the intercession of the Blessed Virgin Mary,
    Mother of God,
pour into these your servants
the strength to persevere,
so that by following you faithfully
they may fulfill the vows which they now renew.

We ask this through Christ our Lord.

R.   Amen.

IV. ANOTHER SOLEMN PRAYER OF BLESSING OR CONSECRATION OF THE PROFESSED

159.   Lord God, creator of the world and Father of humankind,
we honor you with praise and thanksgiving,
for you chose a people from the stock of Abraham
and consecrated them to yourself,
calling them by your name.
While they wandered in the wilderness
your word gave them comfort
and your right hand protection.

When they were poor and despised,
you united them to yourself in a covenant of love.
When they strayed from your friendship
your mercy led them back to the right way.
When they sought you,
your fatherly care looked after them
until they came to dwell in the land of freedom.

But above all, Father, we thank you
for revealing the knowledge of your truth
through Jesus Christ, your Son, our brother.

Born of the Blessed Virgin,
by dying he ransomed your people from sin,
and by rising again he showed them the glory
that would one day be their own.

When he took his place at your right hand,
he sent the Holy Spirit to call countless disciples

to follow the evangelical counsels
and consecrate their lives to the glory of your name
and the salvation of all humankind.

Today it is right
that your house should echo with a new song of thanksgiving
for these sisters of ours
who have listened to your voice
and made themselves over to your holy service.

Lord, send the gift of your Holy Spirit upon your servants
who have left all things for your sake.
Father, may their lives reveal the face of Christ your Son,
so that all who see them may come to know
that he is always present in your Church.

We pray that in the freedom of their hearts
they may free from care the hearts of others;
in helping the afflicted, may they bring comfort to Christ
suffering in his brothers and sisters;
may they look upon the world
and see it ruled by your loving wisdom.
May the gift they make of themselves
hasten the coming of your kingdom,
and make them one at last with your saints in heaven.

We ask this through Christ our Lord.

R.   Amen.

V. ANOTHER FORM OF BLESSING AT THE END OF THE MASS OF PERPETUAL PROFESSION

160. May the almighty Father make you firm in faith,
innocent in the midst of evil,
and wise in the pursuit of goodness.

R.   Amen.

May the Lord Jesus, whom you follow,
enable you to live out the mystery
of his death and resurrection in your own life.

R.   Amen.

May the fire of the Holy Spirit
cleanse your hearts from all sin
and set them on fire with his love.

R.   Amen.

May almighty God,
the Father, and the Son, + and the Holy Spirit,
bless all of you who have taken part in these sacred celebrations.

R.   Amen.

Additional Texts

I. A SAMPLE FORMULA OF PROFESSION

Each religious community may compose a formula of profession, to be approved by the Sacred Congregation for Religious and for Secular Institutes. For the convenience of religious institutes the following example is given.

1. Candidates for Profession:

I, N.,
for the glory of God,
and intending to consecrate myself more closely to him
and to follow Christ more generously all my life,
with (Bishop N. and) my brothers (sisters) as witnesses
and in your presence, N.,[1]
vow perpetual[2] chastity, poverty and obedience
according to the (rule and) constitutions of N.[3]
With my whole heart I give myself
to this religious community,
to seek perfect charity
in the service of God and the Church,

by the grace of the Holy Spirit
and the prayers of the Blessed Virgin Mary.

2. The person who receives the vows may at a suitable point in the rite (see Part I, no. 70; Part II, no. 77) say the following:

By the authority entrusted to me,
and in the name of the Church,
I receive the vows you have taken
in the community of N.[3]
I earnestly commend you to God,
that your gift of self,
made one with the sacrifice of the Eucharist,
may be brought to perfection.

II. TEXTS FOR MASS

This Mass may be said on any day except the Sundays of Advent, Lent and Easter, solemnities, Ash Wednesday and the weekdays of Holy Week. White vestments may be worn.

1. First religious profession

INTRODUCTORY RITES

> Here am I, Lord; I come to do your will.
> Your law is written on my heart.
> (Psalm 40:8–9)

OPENING PRAYER

Lord,
you have inspired our brothers (sisters)
with the resolve to follow Christ more closely.
Grant a blessed ending to the journey
on which they have set out,
so that they may be able to offer you
the perfect gift of their loving service.

We ask this through our Lord Jesus Christ, your Son,
who lives and reigns with you and the Holy Spirit,
one God, for ever and ever.

R.   Amen.

See Lectionary for Mass, nos. 784–788.

PRAYER OVER THE GIFTS

Pray, brethren . . .

Lord,
receive the gifts and prayers which we offer to you
as we celebrate the beginning of this religious profession.
Grant that these first fruits of your servants
may be nourished by your grace
and be the promise of a richer harvest.

We ask this through Christ our Lord.

R.   Amen.

> *Preface of Religious Profession, page 136, intercessions of the eucharistic prayers, pages 128–131.*

COMMUNION RITE

> Whoever does the will of
> God is my brother,
> my sister, and my mother. (Mark 3:35)

PRAYER AFTER COMMUNION

Let us pray.

> *Pause for silent prayer, if this has not preceded.*

Lord,
may the sacred mysteries we have shared bring us joy.
By their power grant that your servants
may constantly fulfill the religious duties they now take up
and freely give their service to you.

We ask this through Christ our Lord.

R.   Amen.

2. Perpetual profession

A.
INTRODUCTORY RITES

> I rejoiced when I heard them say:
> let us go to the house of the Lord.
> Jerusalem, we stand as pilgrims
> in your court! (Psalm 122:1–2)

OPENING PRAYER

God our Father,
you have caused the grace of baptism
to bear such fruit in your servants
that they now strive to follow your Son more closely.
Let them rightly aim at true evangelical perfection
and increase the holiness and apostolic zeal of your Church.

We ask this through our Lord Jesus Christ, your Son,
who lives and reigns with you and the Holy Spirit,
one God, for ever and ever.

R.   Amen.

See *Lectionary for Mass*, nos. 784–788.

PRAYER OVER THE GIFTS

Pray, brethren . . .

Lord,
accept the gifts and the vows of your servants.
Strengthen them by your love
as they profess the evangelical counsels.

We ask this through Christ our Lord.

R.   Amen.

> *Preface of Religious Profession, page 136.*
>
> *In the eucharistic prayers, the offering of the professed may be mentioned according to the texts below:*

1. For Men

> *a) In Eucharistic Prayer I, the special form of* Father, accept this offering *is said:*

Father, accept and sanctify this offering
from your whole family and from these your servants
which we make to you on the day of their profession.
By your grace
they have dedicated their lives to you today.
When your Son returns in glory,
may they share the joy of the unending paschal feast.

[Through Christ our Lord. Amen.]

> b) *In the intercessions of Eucharistic Prayer II, after the words* and all
> the clergy, *there is added:*

Lord, remember also these our brothers
who have today dedicated themselves to serve you always.
Grant that they may always raise their minds and hearts to you
and glorify your name.

> c) *In the intercessions of Eucharistic Prayer III, after the words* your
> Son has gained for you, *there is added:*

Strengthen also these servants of yours in their holy purpose,
for they have dedicated themselves
by the bonds of religious consecration to serve you always.
Grant that they may give witness in your Church
to the new and eternal life won by Christ's redemption.

> d) *In the intercessions of Eucharistic Prayer IV, the professed may be
> mentioned in this way:*

. . . bishop, and bishops and clergy everywhere.
Remember these our brothers
who unite themselves more closely to you today
by their perpetual profession.
Remember those who take part in this offering . . .

2. For Women

> a) *In Eucharistic Prayer I, the special form of* Father, accept this
> offering *is said:*

Father, accept and sanctify this offering
from your whole family and from these your servants
which we make to you on the day of their consecration.

By your grace
they join themselves more closely to your Son today.
When he comes in glory at the end of time,
may they joyfully meet him.

[Through Christ our Lord. Amen.]

> *b) In the intercessions of Eucharistic Prayer II, after the words* and all
> the clergy, *there is added:*

Remember all these sisters of ours
who have left all things for your sake
so that they might find you in all things
and by forgetting self serve the needs of all.

> *c) In the intercessions of Eucharistic Prayer III, after the words* your
> Son has gained for you, *there is added:*

Lord, strengthen these servants of yours in their holy purpose
as they strive to follow Christ your Son in consecrated holiness
by giving witness to his love in their religious life.

> *d) In the intercessions of Eucharistic Prayer IV, the professed may be
> mentioned in this way:*

. . . bishop, and bishops and clergy everywhere.
Remember our sisters who have consecrated themselves to you
    today
by the bond of religious profession.
Remember those who take part in this offering . . .

COMMUNION RITE

> I am nailed with Christ to the
> cross; I am alive, not by my own
> life but by Christ's life within
> me. (Galatians 2:19–20)

PRAYER AFTER COMMUNION

Let us pray.

> *Pause for silent prayer, if this has not preceded.*

Lord,
as we share these sacred mysteries,
we pray for these your servants

who are bound to you by their holy offering.
Increase in them the fire of your Holy Spirit
and unite them in eternal fellowship with your Son,
who is Lord for ever and ever.

R.   Amen.

SOLEMN BLESSING

May God who is the source of all good intentions
enlighten your minds and strengthen your hearts.
May he help you to fulfill with steadfast faith all you have
    promised.

R.   Amen.

May the Lord enable you to travel in the joy of Christ
as you follow along his way,
and may you gladly share each other's burdens.

R.   Amen.

May the love of God unite you and make you a true family,
praising his name and showing forth Christ's love.

R.   Amen.

May almighty God,
the Father, and the Son, + and the Holy Spirit,
bless all of you who have taken part in these sacred celebrations.

R.   Amen.

B.
INTRODUCTORY RITES

> I will offer sacrifice in your
> temple; I will fulfill the
> vows my lips have promised.
> (Psalm 66:13–14)

OPENING PRAYER

Lord, holy Father,
confirm the resolve of your servants (N. and N.).

Grant that the grace of baptism,
which they wish to strengthen with new bonds,
may work its full effect in them,
so that they may offer you their praise
and spread Christ's kingdom with apostolic zeal.

We ask this through our Lord Jesus Christ, your Son,
who lives and reigns with you and the Holy Spirit,
one God, for ever and ever.

> *See* Lectionary for Mass, *nos. 784–788.*

PRAYER OVER THE GIFTS

Pray, brethren . . .

Lord,
accept the offerings of your servants
and make them a sign of salvation.
Fill with the gifts of your Holy Spirit
those whom you have called by your fatherly providence
to follow your Son more closely.

We ask this through Christ our Lord.

> *Preface of Religious Profession, page 142; intercessions of the eucharistic prayers, as in the preceding Mass.*

COMMUNION RITE

> Taste and see the goodness of the Lord;
> blessed is he who hopes in God. (Psalm 34:9)

PRAYER AFTER COMMUNION

Let us pray.

> *Pause for silent prayer, if this has not preceded.*

Lord,
may the reception of this sacrament
and the solemnizing of this profession bring us joy.

Let this twofold act of devotion
help your servants to serve the Church and humankind
in the spirit of your love.

We ask this through Christ our Lord.

R. Amen.

Solemn Blessing

God inspires all holy desires and brings them to fulfillment.
May he protect you always by his grace
so that you may fulfill the duties of your vocation
with a faithful heart.

R. Amen.

May he make each of you a witness
and sign of his love for all people.

R. Amen.

May he make those bonds
with which he has bound you to Christ on earth
endure for ever in heavenly love.

R. Amen.

May almighty God,
the Father, and the Son, + and the Holy Spirit,
bless all of you who have taken part in this celebration.

R. Amen.

3. Renewal of Vows

*The entrance and communion antiphons, if used, may be taken from
one of the three preceding Masses.*

Opening Prayer

God our Father,
guide of humankind and ruler of creation,
look upon these your servants
who wish to confirm their offering of themselves to you.

As the years pass by,
help them to enter more deeply into the mystery of the Church
and to dedicate themselves more generously
to the good of humankind.

We ask this through our Lord Jesus Christ, your Son,
who lives and reigns with you and the Holy Spirit,
one God, for ever and ever.

R.   Amen.

> *See Lectionary for Mass, nos. 784–788.*

PRAYER OVER THE GIFTS

Pray, brethren . . .

Lord,
look mercifully upon the gifts of your people
and upon the renewed offering by our brothers (sisters)
of their chastity, poverty, and obedience.
Change these temporal gifts into a sign of eternal life
and conform the minds of those who offer them
to the likeness of your Son
who is Lord for ever and ever.

R.   Amen.

Preface of Religious Profession, page 142; intercessions of the eucharistic prayers, as in the preceding Masses.

PRAYER AFTER COMMUNION

Let us pray.

> *Pause for silent prayer, if this has not preceded.*

Lord,
now that we have received these heavenly sacraments,
we pray that your servants will trust only in your grace,
be strengthened by the power of Christ
and be protected with the help of the Holy Spirit.

We ask this through Christ our Lord.

PREFACE OF RELIGIOUS PROFESSION

Priest: The Lord be with you.

People: And also with you.

Priest: Lift up your hearts.

People: We lift them up to the Lord.

Priest: Let us give thanks to the Lord our God.

People: It is right to give him thanks and praise.

Father, all-powerful and ever-living God,
we do well always and everywhere to give you thanks
through Jesus Christ our Lord.

He came, the Son of a Virgin Mother,
named those blessed who were pure of heart,
and taught by his whole life the perfection of chastity.

He chose always to fulfill your holy will
and became obedient even to dying for us,
offering himself to you as a perfect oblation.

He consecrated more closely to your service
those who leave all things for your sake
and promised that they would find a heavenly treasure.

And so, with all the angels and saints
we proclaim your glory
and join in their unending hymn of praise:

Holy, holy, holy Lord, God of power and might,
heaven and earth are full of your glory.
Hosanna in the highest.
Blessed is he who comes in the name of the Lord.
Hosanna in the highest.

NOTES
1. Here are mentioned the name and office of the superior receiving the profession.

2. Or the period of temporary profession.

3. The name of the religious community is mentioned.

III. TWENTY-FIFTH OR FIFTIETH ANNIVERSARY OF RELIGIOUS PROFESSION

This Mass may be celebrated, using white vestments, on all days except the Sundays of Advent, Lent and Easter, solemnities, Ash Wednesday and the weekdays of Holy Week. The entrance and communion antiphons may be taken from one of the preceding Masses.

OPENING PRAYER

God of faithfulness,
enable us to give you thanks
for your goodness to N., our brother/sister.
Today he/she first received from you.
Intensify within him/her your spirit of perfect love,
that he/she may devote himself/herself more fervently
to the service of your glory
and the work of salvation.

We ask this through our Lord Jesus Christ, your Son,
who lives and reigns with you and the Holy Spirit,
one God, for ever and ever.

PRAYER OVER THE GIFTS

Pray, brethren . . .

All-powerful God,
together with these gifts
accept the offering of self
which N., our brother/sister, wishes to reaffirm today.
By the power of your Spirit
conform him/her more truly
to the likeness of your beloved Son.

We ask this through Christ our Lord.

Preface of Religious Profession, page 142.

PRAYER AFTER COMMUNION

Let us pray.

Pause for silent prayer, if this has not preceded.

God of love,
in this joyful anniversary celebration
you have fed us
with the body and blood of your Son.
Refreshed by heavenly food and drink
may our brother/sisters, N., advance happily on that journey
which began in you and leads to you.

Grant this through Christ our Lord.